GREAT PARKS, GREAT DESIGNERS

Paul Rabbitts

AMBERLEY

Acknowledgements

This book has been on the 'to do' list for quite a while, with others taking precedent. I have been conscious that although many individual parks' histories are well known, those that have designed them are not always recognised for the impact of their achievements. I wanted to partly remedy this, and this book is an introduction to many of them. My thanks as always to many, including: Dr Stewart Harding, David Lambert, Drew Bennellick, Shaun Kiddell, Michael Rowan, Connor Stait, Dr Katy Layton Jones, Dr Carole O'Reilly as well as continued inspiration from Page, Plant, Bonham and Jones. Last but never least, thanks to my family: my parents David and Morlene Rabbitts, my children, Ashley, Holly and Ellie Rabbitts and, finally, my ever-tolerant wife, Julie Rabbitts.

To my dear friend, and fellow lover of parks, horticulture and Georgian architecture, Alan Marham.

First published 2017

Amberley Publishing
The Hill, Stroud, Gloucestershire, GL5 4EP
www.amberley-books.com

Copyright © Paul Rabbitts, 2017

The right of Paul Rabbitts to be identified as the Author of this work has been asserted in accordance with the Copyrights, Designs and Patents Act 1988.

ISBN 978 1 4456 7197 0 (print)
ISBN 978 1 4456 7198 7 (ebook)

British Library Cataloguing in Publication Data.
A catalogue record for this book is available from the British Library.

Origination by Amberley Publishing.
Printed in Great Britain.

Contents

Introduction

The history of public parks has been well documented over recent years, with the advent of the Heritage Lottery Fund's 'Urban Parks Programme' and 'Parks for People' funded restoration works. Significant research on the history of our greatest public parks has been carried out and, in many cases, has been published by Friends of Parks or local history societies. Parks historians such as Hazel Conway, Hilary Taylor and Harriet Jordan have eloquently described the evolution of the development of the park movement from Victorian times through the twentieth century and beyond, and have referred to the many great park designers that took up the mantle.

Yet, surprisingly, very little is known about many of them. Certainly, Joseph Paxton, John Nash and James Pennethorne are well documented, as are later park designers, including Thomas H. Mawson, but not much is known about many others. Edward Milner, James Gibson and John James Sexby are often ignored and, despite his output and impact on London, Decimus Burton is rarely acknowledged in relation to his importance to developing the royal parks. Burton himself warrants a full biography, such was his contribution to Regency London, and his impact is still felt today in Hyde Park and Regent's Park. Many of our greatest parks were designed by well-known designers such as Paxton and Milner, but there were equally impressive parks that were laid out by the municipal designers working within the local authorities who were empowered, after subsequent legislation, to plan many of our existing parks. Sexby, Pettigrew and Sandys-Winsch all had major roles to play in some of our greatest cities and there were many more people involved, including park superintendents, borough engineers and surveyors, working at a very local level in a great number of local councils that are barely known.

This book is an attempt to fill this gap in knowledge. The renowned landscape gardeners of Capability Brown, William Kent and Humphry Repton have all contributed to the wider English landscape, but the impact of the great park designers on our towns and cities should be equally acknowledged and recognised. Their legacy remains with us today in what are some of our finest landscapes and our greatest public parks.

Park Design and
Park Designers

Parks varied in size, from small sites to those covering several hundred hectares, and were created out of a wide variety of locations including commons, wasteland, infill and marginal land, such as disused quarries. Some parks were created out of sites that were already partly laid out, as they had previously been private parks and gardens. Some were not fully laid out until many years after they had actually opened as parks. Despite this, it is possible to see certain broad changes in design during the course of the nineteenth century.

The most important influence on landscape design at the beginning of the nineteenth century was Humphry Repton. His theories were to influence John Nash in his revised designs for Regent's Park, and his ideas were developed further well into the nineteenth century by John Claudius Loudon. Many of Repton's principles were influential in early public park design, including those concerning picturesque beauty, variety, novelty, contrast, appropriation and animation. Picturesque beauty encouraged curiosity, and this in turn meant that all significant features of a design should not be immediately visible. Appropriation involved enhancing the apparent extent of an owner's private property, and this too was applied to public parks.

Apart from Repton and Loudon, the other major figure during the first decades of the park movement is, without doubt, Joseph Paxton, with his first public park venture, Prince's Park in Liverpool (1842), which was followed by Birkenhead Park (1842–7). However, it was Crystal Palace Park at Sydenham (1855) that was his most spectacular and influential. One of the problems confronting these early designers, and subsequent later ones, was how to accommodate large numbers of people at the same time, and yet preserve a feeling of space and quiet contact with nature. Another problem concerned the location of an increasing range of activities, such as sports and music, which had to be reconciled with the prevailing contemporary ideals of landscape design – something that James Pennethorne had to struggle with in the early design of Victoria Park in the East End of London. Paxton's design for the Crystal Palace Park became a major influence, while in the 1870s the introduction of French principles of park design at Sefton Park, Liverpool, seemed to point to a solution of accommodating sports and playgrounds. In some instances, designers were chosen by competition, but the role of competitions in this area was not nearly as important as it was in the area of public architecture, and the majority of municipal parks were not designed by competition, which only became more important after 1875.

In the design of municipal parks, it was often the benefactor or the local authority who decided on the facilities to be included, and rarely the designer. The first municipal parks to be designed as the result of a competition were the Manchester parks, and the Public Parks Committee's clearly stated objective was to 'provide the greatest variety of

Hunt's Series

Peel Park, Manchester.

rational recreations for the greatest possible number'. By 1844, they had agreed this was to include gymnasia, one or more fountains of pure water, numerous seats, spaces for active sports such as quoits, skittles and archery, and buildings for refreshments. The committee also expressed and stressed that the designers should pay 'utmost regard ... for the promenading of large numbers of persons,' and to remember that they were sketching 'a park for the public, to be constantly accessible, and not a private pleasure ground'. Over 100 designs were received and differed vastly in style and presentation, making it difficult to compare. Eventually, however, the winner was Joshua Major & Son of Knowstrop, near Leeds. The parks were Queen's Park, Peel Park and Philips Park (although it was only the latter in which Major had a free hand in designing the whole site).

Several alterations were made to Major's designs within two years of the official opening; in particular to Philips Park, the boldest and most romantic of the three parks. The skittle and archery grounds were removed after three years and relocated to the edge of the park, where they were less audible and intrusive. Despite the Manchester Parks Committee being more than content with Major's designs, they did receive criticism in the *Gardeners' Chronicle,* with much being made of 'the profusion of angles' and straight lines to be found in the walks, which was later rebuked by Major. The impact of this was significant, with the movement gathering pace and the momentum being taken up by designers such as James Pennethorne at Victoria Park in London, one which, 'in the variety of its features, and in all its arrangements, may be held to be the best'. It was, however, a while after it opened before it would acquire many of these features, with the 1841 initial design being little more than a sketch, showing sparse planting and no lakes. It was John Gibson, a protégé of Paxton, who would institute many further improvements from 1849 onwards. It was Paxton himself who perhaps had the greatest influence on the laying out of urban and municipal parks across the country, with involvement at Birkenhead, Glasgow, Halifax, Dundee, Dunfermline, Liverpool and London and those that he trained – John Gibson, Edward Milner and Edward Kemp. His influence was to last for several decades.

By the second half of the nineteenth century, changes were brought about with the introduction of Parisian principles to park design in Britain. Jean-Claude-Adolphe, a French engineer and landscape architect, had been laying out parks, including the Bois de Boulogne, the Parc Monceau, the Buttes-Chaumont and the Parc Montsouris, and had been assisted by a young French landscape architect named Edouard André. It was André who introduced Parisian principles of park design to Britain, and the first park in Britain to show that influence was Sefton Park, Liverpool (1872). The competition had been won by him and Lewis Hornblower of Liverpool, who had worked with Paxton on the design of various buildings at Birkenhead Park. Several points were given by the local council, which included preserving the longest vistas in the park, so as to increase its apparent size and positioning, as well as including churches, bandstands and refreshment pavilions as points of interest to terminate those vistas. The walks in the park should provide ready communication to all parts and there should be open ground for cricket and military reviews. Outside the park, the building sites should be arranged so that there was maximum return with the least amount of damage to the ornamental character of the park. It was a difficult site, but the most important innovation was André's layout of the paths and drives within the park. These enclosed a series of open spaces for a variety of activities, which were screened by peripheral planting that offered a solution to the problem of accommodating different sports. This design aspect was to change the way public parks were to be planned, and offer solutions to designers seeking a way to integrate sports and playgrounds into new parks. Alexander McKenzie at Victoria Park, Portsmouth (1878), was one of the first to resolve this issue, as did William Gay in his design for Saltaire Park (1871). This was also shown in the design for Broadfield Park in Rochdale (1871), where the boys' playground and gymnasium was placed at the edge of the park and separated from the rest of the park by a thick belt of planting, which gave privacy to the boys and prevented the playground from becoming 'too prominent an object to those … whose tastes lay in another direction'. The influence of Sefton Park and André's principles of accommodating sports and playgrounds in ellipses and arcs of circles, in order to provide spaces for such facilities as a cricket ground, review ground, bird park, deer park and a botanic garden, was exceptional. And yet, many parks continued to be designed with only a few integrated sports facilities – the exceptions being Stamford Park, Altrincham and West Park, Wolverhampton.

In 1878, William Barron won the competition for the design of Abbey Park in Leicester. Early indications were that all sports were banished from the park, but this was not the case. Although no hint is given on the plan of particular activities, the design included an 'archery ground, lawn tennis, cricket ground, and bowling green', as well as an American garden and rose garden. What was significant was the skill with which Barron accommodated this range of sports within his axial plan.

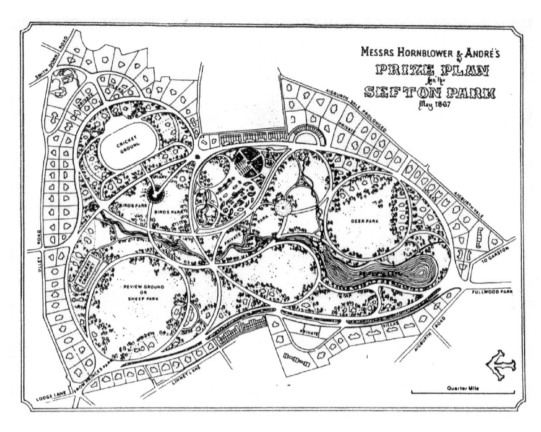

Hornblower and André's prize plan for Sefton Park, Liverpool.

Sefton Park with Palmhouse.

Although such introductions were to affect the later designs of public parks – and none more so than in parks such as Eaton Park in Norwich, designed by Captain Sandys-Winsch – there became a greater emphasis on active sports and the incorporation of such facilities within them, particularly for football and cricket. By 1898, Victoria Park in London had thirty-two cricket pitches and thirty-seven lawn tennis courts. The difficulties of handling such areas in a way that would preserve the feeling of enclosure proved impossible and increasingly the solution was to separate the sports facilities. This was to challenge later park designers such as Alexander McKenzie, Thomas Mawson and those that followed, such as Sexby, Pettigrew and Sandys-Winsch. In many cases, the growth of separate recreation grounds was the response to this problem, as was the growth of football and cricket clubs with their own facilities – both leading to the creation of the playing fields of Great Britain... which is another story yet to be fully told.

Victoria Park, Portsmouth, designed by Alexander McKenzie.

Early Parks, Early Designers

John Nash (1752–1835)

John Nash was born in September 1752, probably in London. His impact on the parks movement may appear at first to be limited, but his influence on later architects and park designers is significant, particularly on James Pennethorne and Decimus Burton who followed him. Nash entered the office of the architect Robert Taylor as an indentured pupil, probably in 1766 or 1767, and was employed first in a 'subordinate capacity' and later as a draughtsman. A 'wild, irregular youth', he worked as a builder and surveyor after leaving Taylor's office. By 1777 Nash had established himself as a speculative builder and surveyor, but, by 1783, he was declared bankrupt.

In or about 1785, Nash moved to Carmarthen. The gentry of south-west Wales were eager to replace or at least remodel their unfashionable and often dilapidated houses in the early 1790s, and Nash succeeded in rehousing several of them in a dignified and unpretentious manner. A more adventurous patron was Uvedale Price of Foxley, Herefordshire, for whom Nash designed a triangular castellated villa on the seafront at Aberystwyth – its bay windows being carefully arranged to command the view. Through Price, Nash became aware of the picturesque aesthetic, which was perhaps the most influential movement in English tastes at the close of the eighteenth century.

By 1796, Nash had become an important figure in Carmarthen society. He lived in a substantial house, which he designed for himself. However, he had already begun to spend an increasing amount of time in London, and he finally left Carmarthen in 1797.

The successful launch of Nash's career as a fashionable London architect owed much to his partnership with Humphry Repton, the best-known English landscape gardener of his time. The two men first met in 1792 at Stoke Edith, Herefordshire, where Nash designed a new parlour in the Etruscan style – his first substantial scheme of interior decoration – but the partnership did not come into existence until 1795, when he took Repton's son John Adey Repton into his office as an assistant. Repton and Nash quickly built up a reputation as designers of rural and suburban villas set in carefully landscaped settings on relatively small estates. In these engaging buildings, Nash made a major contribution to the development of English domestic architecture, experimenting with asymmetrical plans so as to make the most of the views from the house, and, prompted by Repton and the clients, employing a wide variety of styles skilfully adapted to extract the maximum picturesque effect. Nash's partnership with Repton ended acrimoniously in 1800, with Nash having failed – according to Repton – to pay him his share of the 7 per cent fees charged to their joint clients.

By 1800 Nash was on his way to becoming one of the most successful domestic architects in England. This aspect of his work reached its apogee in the building of Blaise Hamlet, near Bristol (1810–11) – an exquisite 'village' of thatched stone cottages for the pensioners of the banker J. S. Harford, set irregularly around a communal green in a wooded setting. Here, with the assistance of George Stanley Repton, Nash employed the architectural vocabulary of the picturesque in an original and totally convincing manner, appealing to the fashionable rural nostalgia of a rapidly urbanising society and anticipating the estate villages, garden suburbs, and even the local authority housing estates of more modern times.

In 1806, while his domestic practice was in full spate, Nash acquired his first official position, as a salaried architect in the Office of Woods & Forests, the government department responsible for managing the Crown Estate. In 1811, he produced his first plans for the long-anticipated development of the Crown land in Marylebone Park, but by then he had been introduced into the circle of the Prince of Wales (from 1811, Prince Regent, and from 1820, George IV). In 1798, while still in partnership with Repton, Nash had designed a conservatory for the prince, and by 1813 Nash was said to be 'in great favour with [him]'. Nash's first architectural commission from the prince was for a thatched cottage *orné,* built around the nucleus of the former lower lodge in Windsor Great Park, and known since the 1820s as the Royal Lodge. It was in 1814 that Nash first attracted notice – some of it unfavourable – as the prince's private architect. He was employed in that year to design a series of temporary structures to celebrate the visit to London by the Allied sovereigns after the treaty of Paris, including a tent-like rotunda (re-erected at Woolwich in 1820 and now the Royal Artillery Museum) in the grounds of Carlton House, the prince's main London residence, and a bridge incongruously surmounted by a pagoda, which perished in a fireworks display, in St James's Park.

When James Wyatt died in 1813, Nash was given temporary responsibility for maintaining the royal palaces and in 1815, when the Office of Works was reorganised,

Nash's Chinese bridge and pagoda in St James's Park, which were erected in commemoration of the peace of 1814.

he was made one of the three 'attached architects', along with John Soane and Robert Smirke. From then on, he virtually gave up taking private commissions. It was while at the Office of Works that Nash became known for one of his greatest achievements – the development that eventually became known as Regent's Park.

This stemmed from the decision by the Office of Woods & Forests in 1810 to implement long-matured proposals for the profitable development of Marylebone Park, on the north-western fringe of London. Backed by the Prince Regent himself, who desired to lend his name to the improvement of London, Nash's plan for Regent's Park, as it became known, was prepared and approved in 1811–12. Drawing on and inspired by earlier plans by the Duke of Portland's surveyor John White, the main feature was to be a large open space laid out on picturesque, Reptonian lines with clumps of trees, an irregular lake and villas scattered among the plantations. This was, at the time, a totally original concept in contemporary urban planning and drew on Nash's love of the picturesque and his experience of designing and building 'rural

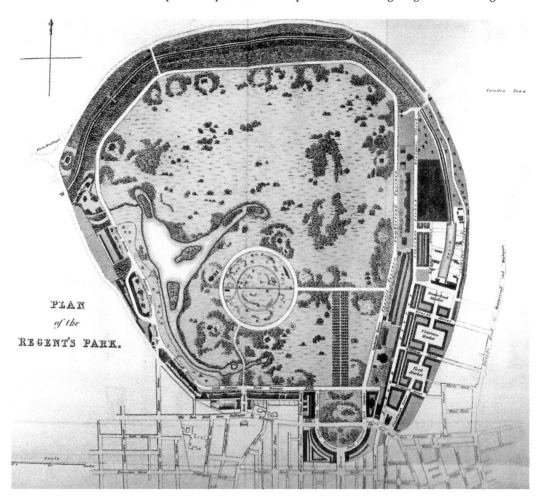

A later plan of Nash's amended design for Regent's Park in 1826.

13

Regents Park, London

Sussex Place in the background of the Regent's Park lake.

and suburban villas set in carefully landscaped settings on relatively small estates'. In this instance he incorporated terraces of middle-class housing that would line the periphery, overlooking the new park, with the Regent's Canal – of which Nash was the leading promoter and largest shareholder – running along the northern perimeter en route from Paddington to the River Thames at Limehouse. A branch of the canal was to lead south to Cumberland basin, serving an area of artisan housing on the eastern fringe of the development, outside the park. A *guinguette*, or pavilion, for the Prince Regent was proposed on a site facing the present Cumberland Terrace but, like most of the desired villas proposed by Nash, this was never built. The drives and plantations were largely completed in 1812, but due to the lack of investors, the canal did not fully open and the building of the terraces, on which the profitability of the whole scheme depended, was delayed until the economy revived in the post-Waterloo years. These palatial-looking structures (including Sussex Place, 1822; Chester Terrace, 1825; and, grandest of all, Cumberland Terrace, 1825) disguise ordinary brick construction behind Nash's gleaming stuccoed façades, and as urban scenery they are second to none. Finally, in 1825, on the north-eastern fringe of the site, spanning the Regent's Canal, Nash laid out the park village – 'more', as he said himself, 'for amusement than profit.' Inspired to some extent by his earlier essay in village planning at Blaise Hamlet, this attractive group of stuccoed villas is one of the main prototypes of the Victorian middle-class suburb.

In nearby St James's Park, Nash was to follow on from his work at Regent's Park – despite the difficulties he had from the outset. Certainly, from the mid-eighteenth century, the fashion for landscape gardening had been incredibly popular. It was Capability Brown

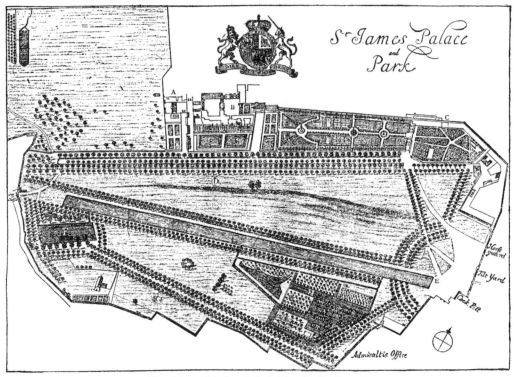

XL. A Map of St. James's Park drawn by Knyff, *c.* 1662.

A Map of St James's Park drawn by Knyff *c.* 1662, prior to Nash's 'best obliteration of avenues'.

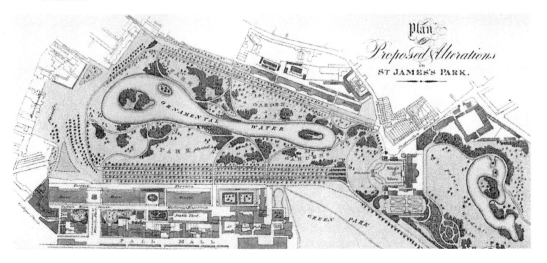

Nash's proposed alterations to St James's Park.

who had set the fashion for 'copying nature', with many of those that followed him going much further. Certainly, the mere sight of a straight canal had become totally unacceptable. The canal in St James's Park was eventually and completely transformed by the time that half the regimented ponds and canals in the country had been twisted and turned into lakes or meres. Capability Brown had more than likely had a hand in the alterations at the time, with Rosamond's Pond being removed; however, fifty years later it was John Nash who planned and executed the most dramatic of works. They began in 1827, and a writer at the time was praiseworthy of the results, describing the transformation as 'the best obliteration of avenues' that had been effected. Although he accepts these dramatic changes, which involved 'a tremendous destruction of fine elms', he is lost in high regard of the 'astounding ingenuity', which 'converted a Dutch canal into a fine flowing river, with incurvated banks, terminated at one end by a planted island and at the other by a peninsula.'

Even before the alterations were started by Nash, the park was noted for being lit with gas lamps – an innovation that created quite a stir. Orders were issued at the same time to shut the gates by ten o'clock every evening. Nash's framework and structure for the dramatically changed St James's Park was the Mall on the north side, with Birdcage Walk on the south, Horse Guards Parade on the east and the new Buckingham Palace to the west. He designed and oversaw the construction of new terraces on the site and grounds of Carlton House, which was no longer used by the monarch. Nash's proposals for several lodges were never executed, and the Mall, which included his proposals to form into a quadruple avenue for riders, carriages, and pedestrians, was invariably adapted in execution.

The Foreign Office from St James's Park.

Thomas Lawrence's portrait of John Nash (1827) at the age of seventy-two. (Courtesy of the Principal, Fellows and Scholars of Jesus College, Oxford)

VIEW IN THE REGENTS PARK, LONDON.

WINTER FASHIONS for 1838 & 39. by B. READ & C? 12, Hart St. Bloomsbury Square, LONDON, and Broad Way, New York, AMERICA.

Fashion plate showing Sussex Place across the lake in 1838–39. Coloured aquatint with etching by B. Read & Co. (Guildhall Library)

17

Gloucester Gate and St Katharine's Hospital *c.* 1829.

The Avenue Gardens, Regent's Park.

St James's Park, summer 2016.

Nash had no children by his second marriage, but from about 1813 he and his wife began to take an interest in her second cousins, the children of Thomas Pennethorne, a Worcester hop merchant, and his wife, Elizabeth. Nash then took one of them, James Pennethorne, into his office as an assistant in place of George Stanley Repton, sending him to the drawing school run by Auguste Charles Pugin and, subsequently, on a two-year-long programme of foreign study and travel in 1824–26 that was clearly intended to groom him as his successor. Nash's career lasted for another nine years before being all but wrecked by political animosity and the death of the king. He was condemned (but vindicated overall) by a new Commons select committee for 'inexcusable irregularity and great negligence' in framing a number of building contracts and accounts.

Nash had a stroke in 1830 and retired to the Isle of Wight, leaving James Pennethorne to manage what remained of his practice in London. He died at East Cowes Castle on 13 May 1835 and was buried on 20 May at the church of St James, East Cowes. Few English architects have had a greater influence on their surroundings than John Nash. He was also able, through the design of Regent's Park, Regent Street and the associated improvements in the West End of London, to make a greater and more beneficial impact on the capital than any other single architect since Christopher Wren.

J. C. Loudon (1783–1843)

John Claudius Loudon was a landscape gardener and horticultural writer, and was born on 8 April 1783 at Cambuslang, Lanarkshire. His impact on the parks movement can be viewed in two ways – firstly, through his writings and publications, with which he competed with Joseph Paxton on a regular basis, but secondly, through the importance of the work he carried out for Joseph Strutt at Derby Arboretum, which was to influence the design of much later Victorian parks.

Loudon began working part-time as an assistant to John Mawer in 1794, a nurseryman and landscape gardener at Dalry. On Mawer's death in 1798 he became a part-time apprentice to Dickson and Shade, nurserymen at Leith Walk, Edinburgh. At the same time he entered the University of Edinburgh, where he studied until 1802, attending lectures on agriculture, as well as classes in botany and chemistry. While at university he developed the habit of staying up two nights a week to study, hence generating his passion for writing. His first publication, a translation of the life of Abelard for an encyclopaedia, took place in 1802. Loudon's first horticultural publication, 'Hints Respecting the Manner of Laying out the Grounds of the Public Squares in London', was published in the *Literary Journal* for 31 December 1803; it revealed him as a follower of Sir Uvedale Price and a critic of Humphry Repton. His first book appeared in 1804, *Observations on the Formation and Management of Useful and Ornamental Plantations*, which was followed in 1805 by *A Short Treatise on Several Improvements Recently Made in Hot-Houses* and in 1806 by a two-volume *Treatise on Forming, Improving, and Managing Country Residences*.

By 13 March 1805 he had been elected to the Society of Arts, and the following year he was made a fellow of the Linnean Society. He had already begun a career as a landscape gardener in 1803, with proposals for improvements to the grounds of Scone Palace, Perthshire, the seat of Lord Mansfield. 1804 saw commissions from the Duchess

J. C. Loudon.

of Brunswick and others for properties in the London vicinity and in Scotland (some of these early commissions he was to describe in his book on Scottish farms in 1811).

In 1806 Loudon moved to 90 Newman Street, London. Several further publications followed and in 1812 he published *Hints on the Formation of Gardens and Pleasure Grounds*, which included designs for formal gardens as well as informal landscapes. By 1826 Loudon had begun publishing the *Gardener's Magazine,* which reached nineteen volumes before it ceased on his death at the end of 1843. It was soon imitated by magazines edited by Joseph Paxton and others, and accusations of plagiarism passed between rival editors. The *Gardener's Magazine* was not Loudon's only venture in periodical publication. Between 1828 and 1836 he edited the *Magazine of Natural History*, and between 1834 and 1839 the *Architectural Magazine*, which provided the young John Ruskin's first opportunity at publication. In 1830 Loudon also launched a folio publication, *Illustrations of Landscape-Gardening and Garden Architecture*, but this was poorly subscribed to and was discontinued after its third number in 1833.

As a landscape gardener, he contributed little on the ground, preferring to pontificate through his writings, and yet, Loudon designed a small public garden at an unnamed location in 1835, which has been identified as Gravesend, Kent. The site, although built over in the 1870s, marked his practical involvement with the movement in favour of creating public walks and gardens for the country's congested towns. In 1839 came his most significant commission and an opportunity to translate many of his 'visions' into reality. He was commissioned by Joseph Strutt to design a public garden for Derby; the 11-acre Derby Arboretum was opened in 1840, and Loudon published a book about its design in the same year.

In the early part of the nineteenth century the site of the proposed arboretum was a private pleasure and kitchen garden belonging to Joseph Strutt. Strutt was the third son of Jedediah Strutt, a prosperous Derby industrialist who had pioneered the improvement of the stocking frame. Strutt lived at Darley Abbey from 1818 until the death of his only son and his wife in about 1840, whereupon he returned to live in St Peter's Street, Derby. In May 1839, Strutt commissioned a plan from Loudon for a garden he owned near his home to be laid out for public use. The commission required various existing features to be retained, including some mature trees, a flower garden, a cottage and an ivy-clad tool shed: these features had formed part of the earlier garden in which Strutt's children had played. The public garden was not to be expensive to maintain, a factor which encouraged Loudon to propose an arboretum. Work on laying out the new public garden commenced in July 1839 with the formation of earth mounds and the planting of the new trees and shrubs. Loudon combined axial symmetry with informal paths and planting. A broad central walk provides the spine of the design and at the junction of a central gravel walk and the main cross walk stood a statue on a pedestal, since 'a straight walk without a terminating object is felt to be deficient in meaning'. Pavilions providing seats and shelter performed the same function at the ends of the cross walks. The subsidiary walks took the visitor around the periphery of the site, and the undulating ground and planting promoted the illusion

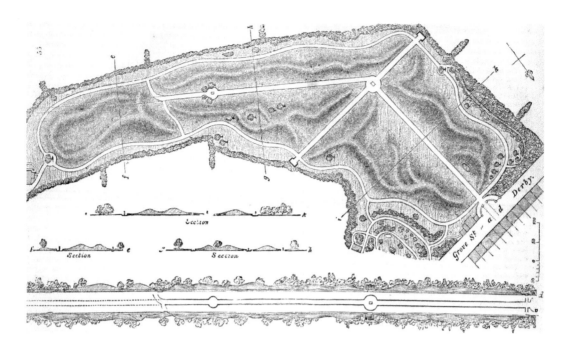

A plan of Derby Arboretum by Loudon.

of solitude and obscured the boundary, thus concealing the apparent extent of the site. Unlike later park designers, Loudon was not required to incorporate a wide range of facilities within his design. There were 350 seats in the Arboretum and Loudon gave detailed instructions on how they should be placed, so that the extent of the park was not made obvious. Seats also had to face a view or a feature, with some being placed in shade and some in the full sun. Loudon was concerned with security as well, and decided that seats placed on grass should be backed by trees and shrubs so that no one could easily come up close to or behind them.

The arboretum was opened on 16 September 1840, when it was handed over to a board of trustees as a place of recreation for the inhabitants of Derby who might 'enjoy a rare opportunity of expanding their minds by the contemplation of nature'. Strutt did not provide an endowment for the upkeep of the arboretum, believing that, while it should be open to the general public free of charge on Sunday afternoon and Wednesday, on other days 'a small sum should be required from persons entering the garden'. A system of annual subscription was also implemented.

The last direction in which Loudon directed his talents was in the creation of cemeteries. In 1842, with Edward Buckton Lamb as his architect, he designed the Histon Road cemetery in Cambridge, which was laid out on a strict grid plan to facilitate the location of graves, and was planted with specimen trees, mostly evergreens, which he arranged geometrically. A series of articles on cemetery design, criticising various aspects of the layout and management of the new cemeteries that had been opened in the preceding twenty years, and advocating grid layout and evergreen planting, was published in the *Gardener's Magazine* in 1843 as 'On the Planting, Managing, and Laying out of Cemeteries'. Loudon's financial difficulties led him to accept two commissions for

The Arboretum, Derby.

Autumn in the Arboretum.

Autumn in the Arboretum and the mounds created by Loudon.

cemeteries in 1843 – one for a private company (Bath Abbey Cemetery) and one for a local authority (Southampton Cemetery). He saw neither project to completion, and his plans for Southampton were the subject of much controversy with the council.

Ill health had dogged Loudon for many years. While working simultaneously on plans for Coleshill House, Berkshire, and his two cemeteries, he was taken ill on a visit to the Isle of Wight. Not long after returning to London he died at his home, 3 Porchester Terrace, on 14 December 1843; his death certificate attributed his death to chronic bronchitis. He was buried in Kensal Green cemetery on 21 December.

Decimus Burton (1800–1881)

Decimus Burton was yet another architect who was to have a major impact on the provision of parks, and in London especially. He was born on 30 September 1800 as the tenth son of James Burton, a builder and speculative developer. Decimus was to benefit greatly from his father's success and wealth, which enabled his own professional life to develop comfortably. However, the facts that he was not articled to an architect, nor did he go on the grand tour early in life, were considered anomalies in the training of an architect. As a consequence of this, Burton stood, unfairly, outside the growing circle of professionally educated practitioners in early nineteenth-century Britain. During his time as his father's assistant, Decimus received drawing lessons from George Maddox but, more importantly, he learned about efficient working practices from his father's productive career. The qualities of efficiency, professionalism and an educated sensitivity

Right: A young Decimus Burton Esquire.

Below: The hot-house at the Royal Botanic Gardens, Regent's Park.

Regent's Park.   The Hot-house, Royal Botanic Gardens.

to the wider implications of design for the creation of distinct urban environments, rather than any kind of 'genius', are the hallmarks of Decimus Burton's architecture. He is, in many academics' views, vastly underrated and under-valued.

Burton's training at the Royal Academy comprised of lectures delivered by John Soane, professor of architecture, and the use of casts as models, from which he was to draw and learn about the architecture of the ancients. Both lessons remained an important influence on Burton. Although Burton travelled to France and Spain, about which little is known, the absence of an educative grand tour early in his career meant that his books and casts were his sources for design. This goes some way towards explaining the rather stiff and academic character of his architecture.

Despite his lack of direct contact with antique architecture, Burton was widely fêted in the contemporary press as a significant exponent of the Greek revival style and his individual works – including the Hyde Park screen (1823–25), which was heralded as the 'new Propylaea', and the Athenaeum (1827–30) – were much praised. Both of these buildings were decorated with a copy of the Panathenaic procession from the Parthenon frieze, executed by the sculptor John Henning.

One of the most problematic areas of Burton's early career was his relationship with John Nash, the favoured architect of George IV. It has been assumed that Burton worked in Nash's office, but there is no evidence to support this. Rather, his working relationship with Nash began through his father's work on the Regent Street and Regent's Park projects, for which Nash was the architectural overseer. In this, James Burton enabled the building work and Decimus provided the architectural styling. This relationship reveals Burton's developing independence as he emerged as the dominant force in the construction of these distinctive urban spaces. As an independent practitioner, Burton was responsible for much of the architecture and landscaping of Regent's Park, where he worked not only with his father, but also with other developers and organisations. In addition to the Colosseum, he was also responsible for the design and layout of the Zoological Society gardens (1826–41) within Regent's Park and those of the Botanical Society (1840–59), which were also within Regent's Park. Many of the villas that contributed to the architectural character of the park were designed or redesigned by Burton. These include: The Holme (1818), built for his father; South Villa (1819); the

The Screen on Hyde Park Corner.

Marquess of Hertford's villa; and Grove House, where Greenough lived until his death in 1856. Hanover Lodge was designed by Burton for the Napoleonic veteran Sir Robert Arbuthnot, who took up residence in 1827; St John's Lodge, owned by John Mabberley MP, was let in 1829 to Marquess Wellesley, who employed Burton to enlarge it. The last villa to be built in the park was a large house for Sir James Holford (built 1832–33), for which Burton drew on his earlier design for Holwood House in Kent.

Burton's most important work in London was carried out for the Office of Woods and involved yet another royal park that needed remodelling. This began at the conjunction of Hyde Park, St James's Park and Green Park, at the area known as Hyde Park Corner, and shows him to be one of the main executants of the vision of George IV and his ministers of London as a royal city rivalling its European counterparts. In collaboration with the king and his chief officials, Burton planned to create an urban space dedicated to the celebration of the Hanoverian dynasty, to national pride and to the nation's heroes. The project, which evolved in the 1820s, comprised creating two aligned entrances – the arch at Constitution Hill into Green Park and the Hyde Park screen at Hyde Park Corner. These two entrances would form part of a processional route for the monarch from Buckingham Palace to Hyde Park, which was becoming an increasingly significant public space. The work required the removal of the toll gate, which had defined Hyde Park Corner as the entrance to London from the west, and the levelling of the approach road to make the site more amenable to development. This set piece of urban planning was, however, never completed. The arch at Constitution Hill was left devoid of decorative

LONDON. THE WELLINGTON ARCH.

The Wellington Arch.

sculpture as a result of the moratorium in 1828 on public building work, and was used instead – much to Burton's chagrin – as a plinth for an oversized, and much ridiculed, equestrian statue of the Duke of Wellington by Matthew Cotes Wyatt (which was later removed to Aldershot). In 1883, the arch at Constitution Hill was turned and re-sited to make way for increased traffic, and Burton's two aligned entrances were thus knocked off their axis.

In 1825, Burton began work on the three royal parks that met at Hyde Park Corner. The spread of the city westwards highlighted the social and political importance of these open landscapes. Positive reactions to Regent's Park as a public open space, to which Burton had made a substantial contribution, encouraged him to make a similar statement about urban planning in his designs for Hyde Park and Green Park; these, though in a poor state, bordered and halted the development of fashionable West London. Repair, replanting and much remedial work were necessary alongside Burton's new designs for the Stanhope, Grosvenor, and Cumberland gates. More ambitious plans for the parks that were not realised include the dramatic circular Bayswater Gate and Lodge, as well as an entrance to Green Park from Piccadilly based on a Greek temple design. In their relationship to the new royal residence, Buckingham Palace, Hyde Park, Green Park and St James's Park collectively constituted the kind of landscape that surrounded country houses. Owned by the Crown, these parks were redesigned by Burton both as a way of enhancing the status of the monarch and the nation, and as a way of ensuring effective communication between important public buildings. In 1850–51, Burton returned to work on Buckingham Palace, where he was responsible for the removal of Nash's Marble Arch, then positioned to face the building, to its present site, and he was also responsible for the subsequent enclosure of the palace forecourt.

Burton's last major public commission took him to Dublin, where he was employed by the reformed Irish board of works to redesign Phoenix Park, which lies to the north-west of the centre of Dublin. The scale and significance of the work, carried out between 1832 and 1849, is comparable to that carried out in the royal parks in London and included new lodges, entrances and landscaping. Burton played a central role in the work. Other

Hyde Park Corner and the Screen today.

28

figures involved in its implementation and execution, many of whom were key figures in contemporary politics, had also worked on the royal parks in London.

Alongside his public career, Burton carried out many private commissions in addition to the villas in Regent's Park. Later in his career, Burton became involved with innovative glasshouse designs, including the Palm House (1845–48) and the Temperate House (1859–62) at Kew Gardens, where he also designed the Museum of Economic Botany. His earlier work on the 'Great Stove', or conservatory, at Chatsworth, for the 6th Duke of Devonshire caused much controversy, as a public row blew up between Burton and his collaborator Joseph Paxton about who had been responsible for the design. Although opinion favoured Paxton, Burton expressed his frustration and anger at the appropriation of his work in letters to his close friend John Wilson Croker. Burton retired from professional life in 1869 (his nephew Henry Marley Burton taking over his practice) and lived quietly at his houses in St Leonards, Sussex, and 1 Gloucester Houses, Kensington, where he died twelve years later, on 14 December 1881. He was buried in Kensal Green Cemetery.

Robert Marnock (1800–1889)

Robert Marnock was one of the most outstanding Victorian horticulturists and designers of gardens of his time. He was considered by his contemporaries to be the best exponent of the gardenesque school of landscape gardening – a style originated in 1832 by John Claudius Loudon, in which the plants of the garden were the centre of attention, rather than the preconceived garden design. Marnock was born on 12 March 1800 at Kintore, Aberdeenshire. He is first recorded as a gardener at Bretton Hall, Yorkshire (now the Yorkshire Sculpture Park), where he became head gardener between 1829 and 1933, and it was while he was there that he entered and won the competition to design the Sheffield Botanic Garden.

Thomas Dunn, the then Master Cutler of Sheffield, called a public meeting in June 1833 following a petition signed by eighty-five local residents concerned about the lack of public open spaces and facilities to promote both healthy recreation and self-education in Sheffield. It was resolved, at the meeting, to develop a Botanical Garden. By 1834, the society had managed to raise £7,500 through shares, and, having taken practical advice from Joseph Paxton at Chatsworth and Joseph Harrison of Wortley Hall, they purchased 18 acres of south-facing farmland from the Wilson family, the snuff makers. The society then advertised a competition for laying out the grounds, and the submitted plans were judged by experienced gardeners including Paxton, Cooper (Wentworth), Walker (Banner Cross) and Wilson (Worksop Manor). Marnock was appointed to design the gardens and act as their first curator. He laid out the gardens in the gardenesque style, where each plant was displayed to perfection in scattered plantings. The runner up in the competition, Benjamin Broomhead Taylor, was appointed as the architect for the buildings.

The gardens were finally opened on 29 and 30 June, and 4 and 5 July 1836, with more than 12,000 people visiting. The gardens were only open to the general public on about four gala days per year; otherwise, admission was limited to shareholders and annual subscribers. Marnock was appointed at an annual salary of £100. He became the first curator of the gardens in 1836 and also acted as a landscape consultant for the Sheffield

Sheffield Botanical Gardens and the Pavilions. The wrought iron glazing bars, which have survived, were based on a system invented by J. C. Loudon.

The Botanical Gardens, designed in the gardenesque style.

General Cemetery, across the valley from Sheffield Botanical Gardens, which opened in 1836 and is considered a nationally outstanding example of a Victorian cemetery.

Marnock then worked as a nurseryman at Hackney until 1839, and in 1840 he moved on to lay out the gardens of the Royal Botanic Society of London in Regent's Park and was appointed as the garden's curator on the advice of John Claudius Loudon: 'Mr Marnock has evidently an excellent taste in landscape gardening, and may be regarded, in this point of view, as a valuable acquisition to the part of the country in which he is situated.' Marnock won the competition to design the garden, with his design keeping 'the number of walks to a minimum', while leaving 'the central mass of the garden an open lawn' and screening 'the specialist gardens behind shrubberies and an elevated rockwork; the garden was bisected by a straight walk leading to the great conservatory, thus imposing an axis of symmetry'. It led to the recognition of Marnock as one of the leading landscape gardeners of the day. During much of his time at Regent's Park, he was aided by the Irishman William Robinson, most of whose early work after his arrival in England was carried out under Marnock's aegis. As curator of the garden, Marnock also successfully managed the exhibitions at the Royal Botanic Society's gardens. He relinquished his post there in 1862, after which date he practised as a landscape gardener until 1879.

Marnock was to return to Sheffield for two further commissions, which included Weston Park in 1873. Weston Park was the first municipal park in Sheffield and developed from the grounds of Weston Hall, which was converted into Sheffield City Museum. In July 1873, Weston Hall and its grounds, built by Thomas Harrison, a Sheffield saw-maker, were purchased from the Harrison Trust by the Sheffield Corporation under the Public Health Act 1848. The grounds were modified for use as a public park by Marnock, who used much of the existing layout in his design. The park – the first to be bought with public funds and to be made available to the people of Sheffield – was opened in September 1875.

Further commissions were to follow, particularly in the south of England. In 1877, the council in Hastings commissioned Marnock to 'provide the bulk of the trees and shrubs which are likely to be required for the public park' for what was to become Alexandra Park, and a limit of £250 was set. Alexandra Park became renowned for its collection of trees, both rare and common. Over 2,000 trees of about 400 different kinds (including forms and cultivars) were grown in the park, and there were more in the adjacent woods. The cultivation of rare species seems to have begun during the laying out of the main part of the park between 1878 and 1882, with collections of oaks, limes and maples being established, along with a bank of beech cultivars and an avenue of different hollies. Alexandra Park was officially opened on 26 June 1882 by the Prince and Princess of Wales (Princess Alexandra). However, one of his finest parks was in nearby Tunbridge Wells – what became Dunorlan Park.

The design for Dunorlan Park was in Marnock's 'pictorial gardenesque' style and was planted predominantly with exotic planting planned for colour, bold effect and botanical variety. The trees and shrubs were grouped on the sweeping lawns, positioned to control and exploit the views. The design has been little altered and many fine trees survive within the pleasure grounds and the park, including large, mature specimens or groups of oak, lime, sweet chestnut, beech, Scots pine and sycamore, along with mature cedar,

Weston Park, Sheffield.

The Glass Pavilions in 2017, seen after restoration that was funded by the Heritage Lottery Fund.

deciduous cypress, deodars and Ponderosa pine specimens. A less well known work by Marnock was Grosvenor Recreation Ground, near Quarry Road, Tunbridge Wells, which was opened in 1889 by Mayor John Stone-Wigg.

Perhaps the most distinctive feature of a Marnock landscape is the importance, even on small sites, of a broad sweep of high-quality lawn and the position of trees in relation to it. Marnock's landscapes were designed to be maintained to a high standard. At places like Dunorlan, with wealthy clients, elaborate landscapes were immaculately kept. On the other hand, at Sheffield Botanical Gardens a small staff maintained standards by avoiding time-consuming effects. Layouts like the drifts of path-side planting at Regent's Park and Sheffield Botanical Gardens are in contrast to the dotting of individual plants within grassland, and were easier to maintain, as well as being more attractive.

Marnock retired in 1879, leaving his business to Joseph Weston, although he continued to give professional advice on landscape gardening until the spring of 1889, in which year he designed his last private garden, that of Sir Henry Peck at Rousdon, near Lyme Regis. He died at his home, 1B Oxford and Cambridge Mansions, Marylebone Road, London, on 15 November 1889. In accordance with his wishes, his body, after a religious service, was cremated at Woking, and his ashes were deposited in his wife's grave at Kensal Green Cemetery on 20 November.

James Pennethorne (1801–1871)

Sir James Pennethorne, an architect, was born on 4 June 1801 in Worcester. He was educated in Dr Simpson's academy, but in 1820 he took the place of his elder brother, Thomas, as a clerk in the London office of the architect John Nash, whose second wife was his second cousin; the legend that he was an illegitimate son of the Prince of Wales

James Pennethorne.

33

(later King George IV) by Mrs Nash cannot be substantiated. Nash's influence was crucial in shaping Pennethorne's career. It was Nash who arranged for him to be taught drawing by Augustus Charles Pugin in 1821–23. In October 1824, Pennethorne embarked on two years of foreign travel and study, which was financed by Nash and clearly intended to establish him as his successor.

Pennethorne corresponded regularly with Nash while abroad and, on his return, he resumed his position in the older architect's office, becoming his chief assistant in 1828. In this capacity, he supervised the last of the metropolitan improvements designed, under an Act of Parliament of 1826, to link the newly created Regent Street to Trafalgar Square and the Strand. He was involved in the construction, and perhaps also to some extent in the internal design, of Nash's new state rooms at Buckingham Palace and when Nash retired to the Isle of Wight, he took charge of his London office in 1830. One of the works he had in hand was the completion of Park Village West, one of Nash's speculations to the north-east of Regent's Park, and here Pennethorne supervised the building – and may have been involved in the design – of some of the houses.

Pennethorne's independent career got off to a very slow start, with him designing a number of buildings, including a handful of country houses and churches, but failing to win any of the competitions he entered. Despite being recommended by Nash to the Commissioners of Woods & Forests in 1834, he gained no official work until 1839, when he was appointed architect and surveyor to the commissioners for a new phase of metropolitan improvements designed to drive new streets through slum areas in or near the heart of London; the appointment was held jointly with Thomas Chawner, who retired in 1845. An architect primarily, Pennethorne was involved in two of the most important parks projects in London, which remain today as two of the finest parks in the country – Victoria Park and Battersea Park.

The need for new parks was most obvious in the crowded streets and squalid courts of the East End. The question of creating a park here was raised in 1838 by Joseph Hume, the radical MP for Middlesex and a member of the 1838 Select Committee on Metropolitan Improvements. Hume had been interested in the provision of parks for the poor since 1832. His appeal for a park in the East End was reinforced by the publication of the first report of the Registrar of Births, Deaths and Marriage in 1839. The creation of a new park in the East End could be presented as a token of their concern to help eradicate some of the worst evils of modern urban life. Pennethorne, who had already prepared schemes for the new streets, was an obvious choice to investigate sites. His report, presented in April 1841, marked the first stage in the formation of what became Victoria Park – the first park specifically intended for the poor in any capital city. Pennethorne suggested two possible sites with the Commissioners of Woods, with the site at Bonners Fields being eventually chosen. The first plan for laying out the ground was submitted with the signatures of Pennethorne and Chawner in June 1841. The design showed a rudimentary layout of trees in clumps, bounded by a drive around the perimeter, beyond which houses were arranged in terraces, 'as in the Regent's Park'. Pennethorne at the same time persuaded the commissioners to turn down proposals for a private zoo on the grounds that it would encourage 'fireworks and evening assemblages'. By 1844, Pennethorne

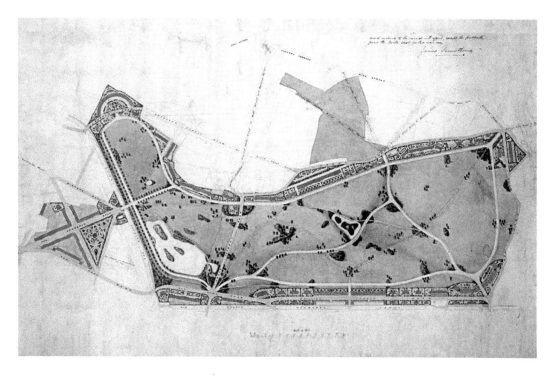

Pennethorne's 1846 plan. (National Archives, ref LRRO1/2036/11)

had prepared designs for the approach roads and for the main entrance lodge. The lodge and gate piers were designed in the florid Jacobean manner, which Pennethorne was currently recommending as a model for the development of New Oxford Street. The lodge, destroyed in the Second World War, was a substantial two-storied red brick building with a low tower capped by a parapet with strapwork ornament and obelisks. Its presence gave an elevated aristocratic character to the park, distinguishing it from a mere piece of common ground and enabling some control to be kept over who came in and out.

Pennethorne's general plan showing the proposed layout of drives, paths and plantations was accepted by the Commissioners of Woods & Forests, with the detailed management of the planting being placed in the hands of Samuel Curtis. The ground was thrown open to the public as work proceeded, and according to *The Times*, 25,000 people went there on Good Friday 1846. The main change to Pennethorne's original plans for the layout came with the decision to form a lake, to 'suit the present forms and levels of ground, and to produce as much variety of scenery as may be obtained in the limited space without any great increase of cost'. There was some popular pressure for a boating lake, and Pennethorne reminded the commissioners of 'the good effect which rational amusements produce on the lower orders – and the ornamental water in St James's Park, Hyde Park and the Regent's Park have been the source of such enjoyment to the Public as to induce a general feeling that ornamental water is almost an integral and indispensable part of a Royal Park'.

In his final design for the park, Pennethorne achieved a satisfying balance between formality and irregularity. The broad 'carriage drive' around the perimeter and the straight avenue leading north across the park from the entrance gates towards Hackney imparted

Victoria Park boating lake.

a note of elevated grandeur that was noticeably absent from most of the East End. The drives and pathways were liberally planted with trees and shrubs, which conveyed a sense of expansiveness, and further variety came from the lake, which was dotted with islands to give the effect of 'intricacy' so admired by Humphry Repton and his successors. The purchase, on Pennethorne's recommendation, of a Chinese pagoda of iron for one of the islands added to the picturesque charm. A second lake in the northern portion of the park, approved by the commissioners in mid-1847, was eventually used for bathing, despite objections from Pennethorne that it would 'quite destroy the value of the Park as a place of residence'. A gymnasium and a second boating lake followed later. Like Nash, Pennethorne was no plantsman, relying instead on Curtis, who proved negligent in his duties. John Gibson was then appointed in his place, making few alterations to Pennethorne's plans.

Victoria Park was a great success. By the late 1850s, an estimated 60–70,000 people were visiting it each Sunday. One commentator wrote:

> The rich and powerful no longer deem the poor beneath their contempt ... No nobler monument exists of the kindly disposition which now generally prevails, for ameliorating the condition of the operative classes; no surer antidote is found to the incendiary harangue, which would make the humble discontented with their governors, than Victoria Park.

The creation of Victoria Park raised the expectations of the poorer inhabitants of the rest of London. Pennethorne and Chawner were asked to investigate possible sites for

Boating on the lake in Victoria Park.

parks in other parts of London as early as the autumn of 1841. They suggested four sites north of the Thames and six to the south. The need to the south seemed greater and here the architects suggested making a park on 55 acres of ground, which included Kennington Common – 'a dreary place of waste land, covered partly with short grass, and frequented only by boys flying their kites or playing at marbles'. Plans foundered in 1842 but land was finally acquired by the government and laid out as a park in 1852–53, after Pennethorne had made 'detailed plans and schedules' for the site. The outcome was significantly different to his proposals, with the final park being a 'pretty promenade ... intersected by broad and well-kept gravelled walks bordered with flower-beds'.

Pennethorne played a much more significant role in the formation of the other government-sponsored park in south London, at Battersea Fields. The creation of Battersea Park was first proposed in 1843 when the property developer Thomas Cubitt, and the local vicar, the Honourable Reverend Robert Eden, reported to Queen Victoria's Commission for Improving the Metropolis. In 1846, an Act of Parliament was passed that authorised the formation of a park on a part of Battersea Common and Battersea Fields, which included the pleasure grounds of the Red House inn. The question of designing and funding the park was taken up seriously by the commissioners in 1845. Thomas Cubitt was not prepared to pay for the park himself. The vicar of Battersea had already prepared a plan for the 315-acre site but the commissioners did not trust his estimate of the cost and turned to Pennethorne, who was asked to prepare a detailed plan of his own, under which a third of the ground would be used for houses. Pennethorne sketched out the bones of what we see in the park today, including a circular carriage drive, lake and riverside promenade, but with villas placed within the perimeter of the park. Convinced that the scheme would make a profit, the commissioners approved the proposal and in 1846 an Act of Parliament was passed that authorized the Commissioners of Woods & Forests to borrow £200,000 for making the park and £120,000 for the construction of Chelsea Bridge. Pennethorne set about securing the land from the smallholders, which proved a protracted and expensive process, as once the decision to create a park was made public, many smallholders held out for as much as ten times the value of the land. With the original budget exceeded before work had begun, the government voted a rescue package of additional funds in 1854.

Pennethorne's design dramatically changed the existing topography of Battersea Fields and created an entirely new landscape with raised contours, artificial lakes and cascades, formal carriage drives and promenades. The natural landscape was to be superseded by an artificial, ornamental landscape, designed to impress and delight. By 1856, rebutting concerns over expenditure, Pennethorne assured the First Commissioner of Works that:

> In a few years, after the plantations shall have formed, there will probably not be a Park near London presenting more attractions of Scenery or more sources for the enjoyment and recreation of the Public than Battersea Park – and the locality altogether, instead of being a hot bed of malaria, fever and crime, will be, as I firmly believe, a Suburb worthy in every respect of the West End of London.

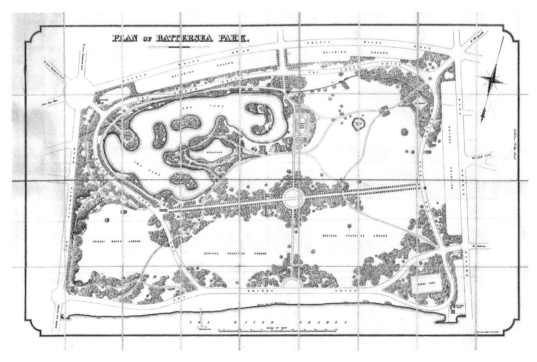

A plan of Battersea Park, 1861.

Battersea Park avenue and promenade. (Peter Jeffree)

The Burdett-Coutts Drinking Fountain in Victoria Park, which was built in 1862. (Peter Jeffree)

Hall was unimpressed, and when Pennethorne refused to accept responsibility for overspending on the original budget, relieved him of further control of the project. The responsibility for further developing the park was given to John Gibson, the park's first superintendent.

Pennethorne's remaining and later career is littered with the debris of abandoned projects for public buildings in London. His post as salaried architect and surveyor to the government was abolished following a further reorganisation of the Office of Works by Gladstone's First Commissioner of Works, A. H. Layard, and he retired on 30 June 1870. He was given a royal gold medal by the Royal Institute of British Architects in 1865 and a knighthood in November 1870. His career was, in some respects, a frustrating one, plagued as it was by political interference and perhaps also by a deep-seated failure to escape fully from the shadow of his mentor, John Nash.

But Pennethorne's long-term legacy was greater than the relatively modest tally of his buildings might suggest. He was one of the most accomplished classical architects of his age and, as a designer of new streets and with his parks, he played a crucial part in the shaping of mid-Victorian London. Pennethorne moved to Worcester Park House, Long Ditton, Malden, Surrey, in 1865, and it was there that he died from a heart condition on 1 September 1871. He was buried in Highgate cemetery.

Joseph Paxton (1803–1865)

Without a doubt, Sir Joseph Paxton was responsible for some of the greatest parks in the country, but his most significant contribution was what he started and influenced – the beginning of the great parks movement – which was the inspiration for those that followed him, in particular John Gibson, Edward Milner and Edward Kemp. He was a landscape gardener and architect, and was born on 3 August 1803 at Milton Bryan in Bedfordshire as the youngest of eight children.

Paxton attended the free school at Woburn, and was allegedly a garden boy to Sir Hugh Inglis at Milton Bryan Manor. At the age of about fourteen he was placed under his older brother John, the gardener at Battlesden, the estate of Sir Gregory Page Turner, where his father had also probably worked. He was later apprenticed for two or three years to William Griffin, the gardener to Samuel Smith of Woodhall Park, Watton, Hertfordshire, who was famous for his skill in fruit growing. In 1821 he returned to Battlesden, where he helped construct an ornamental lake of 13 acres, again under the direction of his brother.

In 1823 Paxton's mother died and he went to work at Wimbledon House, Surrey, where the gardener was another brother, probably James Paxton. He was unsettled there and seems to have left for Lee and Henderson's nursery garden in Kensington. On 13 November that year, recommended by Samuel Smith, he was formally admitted by the Horticultural Society of London as a student gardener at the new experimental garden at Chiswick. He was to excel here and, only a year later, he was promoted to foreman, where he was in charge of the 33-acre arboretum. In 1826, 'owing to some misunderstanding with the authorities of the Society', Paxton intended to go to America, but the Duke of Devonshire intervened. The 6th Duke was the landlord of the society's grounds, and, liking to stroll there and talk to young Paxton, he asked him to be head gardener at Chatsworth, his country house in Derbyshire. The Duke is said to have been impressed with Paxton's bearing and general intelligence, but the deciding factor was his good manners: the Duke was quite deaf, and Paxton took the trouble to speak so that he could hear. It was to be the beginning of one of the greatest partnerships in the history of horticulture. Paxton arrived at Chatsworth on 9 May 1826. The Duke visited nursery gardens with Paxton for the latest plants and took him on garden tours in England and Paris. In 1838, the Duke became president of the Horticultural Society, and that year, accompanied by Paxton, he set off on a seven-month grand tour of Europe, visiting Switzerland, Italy and Turkey. By degrees, a close friendship arose between the Duke and the gardener.

Paxton's responsibilities at Chatsworth steadily increased. He was in charge of the woods in 1830 and of the roads in 1837, and by 1849 he was agent for the Chatsworth estate. Under Paxton's care, Chatsworth became the most famous garden in England. Largely self-taught, Paxton always encouraged the young gardeners (who included John Gibson, Edward Milner, Edward Kemp, and George Eyles) to study and improve themselves. He also designed numerous greenhouses and hothouses, using for many of them his own version of the ridge-and-furrow roof. They culminated in the Conservatory or Great Stove (1836–41), a vast glass building with a double-curved framework of laminated wood, measuring 227 by 123 feet and being 67 feet high. No glasshouse on this scale had ever been built before, and the cautious Duke brought in his architect, Decimus Burton, as a consultant.

Paxton's philosophy on gardening was based on the published works of John Claudius Loudon. However, in the *Gardener's Magazine* of July 1831, Loudon published a long criticism of the Chatsworth gardens, to which Paxton replied two months later in his own paper, the *Horticultural Register*, giving Loudon a mild rebuke. However, by 1835, their quarrel over, Paxton and Loudon remained close and mutually supportive friends. By this time, Paxton was in considerable demand elsewhere, and his portfolio of private work was to expand significantly, including his introduction to the laying out of public parks.

Paxton's private work in the 1840s was in every case undertaken with the Duke's permission. In 1838 he assisted John Lindley in a report on the royal gardens. In 1842, he laid out Prince's Park, Liverpool. For Sir William Jackson, between 1843 and 1847 he created the much greater Birkenhead Park out of a low-lying swamp, together with designs for five ornamental lodges. In 1845–77, he laid out the cemetery at Coventry, with an Italianate lodge and chapels in the Norman and Greek styles. As landscapes, these were all pioneering works that were to influence public park design throughout the nineteenth century.

Paxton's eventual involvement with Prince Albert's Great Exhibition came about almost by chance. The exhibition was due to open on 1 May 1851 but, less than eleven months before that date, the building committee had not yet completed their design for the building in Hyde Park. On 7 June 1850, Paxton, in London, happened to tell a friend, John Ellis, that he had an idea for it; the same day Henry Cole at the Board of Trade said that the committee might still consider a new design. Paxton's drawings, which were presented on 21 June, were based on the as yet uncompleted lily house at Chatsworth, but extended in three dimensions: the building was to cover 19 acres, with the roofs rising in great steps to provide galleries at two levels. The posts and trusses of this huge greenhouse were to be of iron, while the floors, window sashes and roof structure were to be of wood. His design, published in the *Illustrated London News* on 6 July, was reluctantly approved by the committee on 26 July, partly on its merits but also because the contractors had given the lowest of all the tenders. One of the many advantages of Paxton's design was rapid construction, on account of the use of dry components and the standardisation and prefabrication of every part. Paxton's Crystal Palace instantly turned public hostility towards the exhibition into excited anticipation, gaining him a knighthood.

Before the close of the exhibition, Paxton was campaigning for the retention of the Crystal Palace as a winter garden. The public were generally in favour of keeping it in Hyde Park, but the prince wished the building moved, and on 29 April 1852 Parliament voted for just that. Immediately, the directors of the London, Brighton & South Coast Railway floated a company to buy the materials and re-erect the building at Penge Park, near Sydenham, Kent, to be open for the recreation and instruction of the public. Although he was not actually a director of the company, Paxton was indispensable to the whole scheme. Assisted by the contractor John Henderson, he redesigned the building, supervised the winter garden and laid out the terraced garden and park. The initial capital was £500,000 and, in anticipation of high dividends, the enterprise was heavily oversubscribed. But after two years the estimate was greatly exceeded, partly owing to the expenses of the building but, more culpably, due to Paxton's ambitious water gardens,

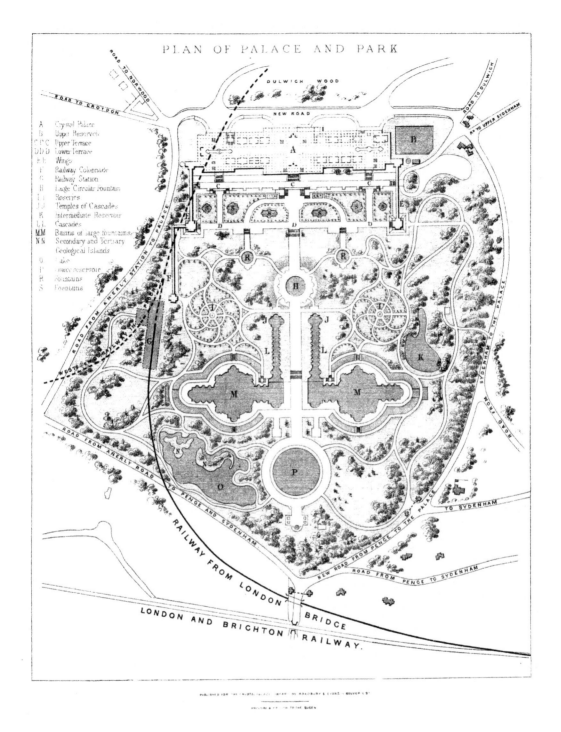

A plan of the Crystal Palace and Park, Sydenham, London, in the 1850s.

The relocated Crystal Palace at Sydenham.

Lithograph published by Day & Son, 1854, showing the Crystal Palace and Park in Sydenham.

44

which were intended to excel those at Versailles. The final estimate was £1.3 million. Share prices fell disastrously, but at the turbulent shareholders' meetings it was not Paxton who was held to blame, but the directors. The Crystal Palace Company never, in fact, recovered from his extravagance.

If the Crystal Palace was an investor's nightmare, it was a great success with visitors. Queen Victoria was enchanted and opened the building, with the winter garden, historic courts and sculpture, on 10 June 1854, and she opened the water gardens on 18 June 1856. In order to attract crowds, the gardens were bedded out with high colour – a scheme reviled by William Robinson and others of the 'natural' gardening school. Nevertheless, despite bankruptcies and other vicissitudes, until the fire of 30 November 1936 Paxton's creation at Sydenham filled the contemporary need for a vast concert hall, exhibition palace and open-air theatre for every kind of great public show.

Paxton continued his architectural career alongside work at the Crystal Palace, which included not just many great houses, but also a number of later public parks, including Baxter Park, Dundee (1862–63); Hesketh Park, Southport; Kelvingrove Park, Glasgow (after 1852); Nottingham Arboretum (1852); People's Park, Halifax (1856); Queen's Park, Glasgow; and Public Park, Dunfermline (1864). However, it was Birkenhead that many still consider his finest work. Birkenhead Park was laid out by Paxton following the Third Improvement Act (Birkenhead) 1843. Paxton was appointed by Sir William Jackson and Edward Kemp, who had worked with Paxton at Chatsworth, Derbyshire, and was recruited to supervise the construction of the park. Another

Crystal Palace Park, in its heyday.

A portrait of Joseph Paxton, holding a copy of *The Magazine of Botany*, 1843. The painting is attributed to Thomas Ellerby (1821–1857).

contact from Chatsworth, John Robertson, designed the lodges around the park with Liverpool architect Lewis Hornblower. Belts of housing around the park boundaries were intended to subsidise the expense of the park. In 1845 Paxton was asked by the commissioners to alter the plans of unsold building plots. At Birkenhead Park, Paxton had introduced lakes as the main focal point of interest in the park. The islands in the lakes prevented the whole expanse of water being taken at a glance, so its extent is not evident. The edges of the lakes were well planted so that they were not obvious and the footpaths around them varied in their distance from the lake edges, so that a variety of views was presented. Mounds and rocky formations created partly out of the lake excavations enclosed the area around the lakes, adding to the privacy of that part of the park and to the variety of the landscape. Open grass contrasted with small-scale, more intimate planting. The areas of formal planting and the layout of the footpaths near the park boundaries reflected the formality of the crescents and terraces of housing facing the park, and contrasted with the informal planting and winding footpaths of the inner areas. Unlike Loudon's Derby Arboretum, there are no straight walks terminated by small buildings within the park.

Following this, he withdrew from further involvement, leaving Edward Kemp in charge of completion. Kemp remained in charge until 1891, serving forty-six years as park superintendent. Opening in 1847, the park was an immediate success, and in 1850

The opening of Birkenhead Park in 1847.

People's Park, Halifax.

Frederick Law Olmsted visited the site. It was Paxton's design that ultimately influenced Olmsted's designs for what became Central Park in New York, which opened in 1858. Ever the workaholic, Paxton's health had deteriorated because of the difficulties with the Sydenham Crystal Palace. Early in 1863 he collapsed, probably from a heart attack, and he never really recovered. His last professional work was to lay out the park at Dunfermline, Fife, which he and Stokes surveyed in September 1864. He died on 8 June 1865 at Rockhills. He was buried at Edensor on 15 June and left a personal estate valued at just under £180,000.

Paxton rose from the ranks to be the greatest gardener of his time, the founder of a new style of architecture and a man of genius, who devoted it to objects in the highest and noblest sense popular. Of his energy and enterprise there is no question. His skill with plants was equalled by a keen eye for the picturesque, which is evident in the design of his many public parks that remain to this day. A magnificent bust of Paxton was erected in Crystal Palace Park in 1873 as a fitting tribute to him.

William Barron (1805–1891)

William Barron was a gardener, nurseryman and landscape gardener active in the nineteenth century. He was born on 7 September 1805 in Eccles, Berwickshire, Scotland. Barron began his gardening career by serving a three-year apprenticeship at Blackadder in Berwickshire, Scotland, and then by entering the Royal Botanic Garden in Edinburgh, Scotland, where he was put in charge of the glasshouses. Following this, he went on to Syon House in Middlesex, England, where he assisted with the planting of a new conservatory.

On 1 March 1830, Barron was appointed gardener to Charles Stanhope, the 4th Earl of Harrington, at Elvaston Castle in Derbyshire, and was instructed to create a new garden. Barron took up his post on 2 August and became particularly concerned with the plantations of numerous species of conifer.

After the Earl's death in 1851, Barron was instructed by Leicester Stanhope, the 5th Earl of Harrington, to construct a commercial nursery in the garden. In 1852, he published *The British Winter Garden: A Practical Treatise on Evergreens*. His first foray into park design was in 1854, with West Park, Macclesfield. Earl Harrington of Elvaston, who also held land close to Macclesfield, provided the services of his principal gardener, William Barron, to design the park, with Barron's foreman, Mr Sturdy, supervising the works. This was followed closely by the Worcester Pleasure Grounds, which were designed by Barron and opened in 1859. They featured an elaborate central fountain with broderie parterres and serpentine walks around them. The Pleasure Grounds were short lived as in 1864 the company went bankrupt and the land was sold for house sites.

In 1862, on the death of the 5th Earl, Barron bought 40 acres for a nursery site in nearby Borrowash, to which he moved in 1865. By 1867 he was joined in partnership by his son. The firm William Barron & Son gained its reputation for plant sales, landscape gardening and the transplantation of large trees, and became a leading provider of public park designs. Barron's many parks included Aberdare Park (1869); Locke Park, Barnsley (1874); Abbey Park, Leicester (1882); and Bedford Park (1888). For the latter, an exhibition

Park Gates, Bedford Park.

Abbey Park, Leicester.

49

of the plans was submitted in response to a competition held in the Bedford Corn Exchange in 1882, the winning entry being that of Messrs W. Barron & Son, landscape gardeners, of the Elvaston Nurseries, Borrowash, Derbyshire. The aim of Barron's scheme was 'a plan which, while providing for the requirements of the Corporation, can be carried out for the modest sum specified, and to give the most pleasing effect obtainable with the materials at our disposal'. A full schedule of the 18,000 assorted trees and shrubs to be planted was provided. The original estimate for the work was just under £4,000, but the final cost, as a result of alterations and additions, amounted to £7,000, not including the buildings. Work began in the spring of 1883 and took two years to complete. The park was opened in July 1888 by the Marquess of Tavistock.

Other park commissions included Brunswick Park, Wednesbury (1887); and People's Park, Grimsby (1883). For the Grimsby park, twenty-four designs were submitted for the tender and the winner, 'William Barron and Son of the Elvaston Nurseries, Derbyshire', was appointed in June 1882, with a design organised around a figure of eight circulation pattern. The park was opened in August 1883. Barron retired in 1881 and died in Borrowash, Derbyshire, on 8 April 1891. His firm was carried on by the family. Among the firm's later commissions were those at Queen's Park, Chesterfield (1893); the Bedford Embankment (1894); and Whitaker Park, Rawtenstall (1900).

John Gibson (1815–1875)

John Gibson was best known as being not only a plant collector, but also a park manager and park designer. Gibson was born in Cheshire and began his career under his father at Eaton Hall, near Congleton, and was eventually apprenticed to Paxton at Chatsworth. Gibson had come to Paxton's attention when he submitted an article to the *Horticultural Register* that was published in October 1832. The following year he arrived to work at Chatsworth from the gardens at Eaton Hall and soon Paxton considered him one of his more 'intelligent gardeners'. It was Gibson that Paxton turned to, sending him on plant-collecting expeditions, citing that Gibson 'has a good knowledge of plants, particularly *orchideae,* is obliging in his manner and very attentive'.

By 1839, with Paxton frequently away on business, Gibson was now often left in charge at Chatsworth. However, by the summer of 1849, Gibson had left Chatsworth to become superintendent of Victoria Park in the East End of London. It was a bold move. As previously covered, Victoria Park was intended to improve the moral as well as the physical conditions of the poor and was laid out on a plan by James Pennethorne. His general plan showed the disposition of drives, paths and plantations and was accepted by the Commissioners of Woods & Forests with the sensible observation that 'the proper direction for the paths will be found to be best ascertained by the Lines, which the Public work out for themselves', and the detailed management of the planting was placed, on the recommendation of Sir William Hooker, director of Kew Gardens, in the hands of Samuel Curtis. The ground was thrown open to the public as work proceeded, and, according to *The Times*, 25,000 people went there on Good Friday 1846.

Like Nash, Pennethorne was not a plantsman, so many of these decisions were left to Curtis, who turned out to be negligent and was dismissed in May 1849. Paxton himself

John Gibson.

was quoted as saying the planting had been done by 'men who did not know the names of half-a-dozen kinds of trees they were planting'. Gibson was given a relatively free hand upon his appointment, making a few alterations to Pennethorne's layout. His first step was to undertake an assessment of the park. Gibson's report indicated that there were a number of construction and management issues to be sorted out. These included:

> Walks completely covered in weeds – an estimate to be sought for cleaning; worn and unsightly path edges, unprotected by iron hurdles; young trees in open areas of the park, including an avenue of cedars, in need of protection from sheep – for which he requested a load of brushwood and tar cordage; cedars to have more substantial guards; rails required for repairing plantation fencing; stakes for standard thorns, roses and other plants requiring support; fencing beside the road from lodge in very bad repair; suggested removal and replacement with iron hurdles.

Finally, he requested a set of tools – pecks, mattocks hoes, rakes, gravel rakes, shovels, scrapes, clipping and pruning shears, bill hooks, axes, saws, knives, scythes, reel and line, grindstone and a small store of nails.

Subsequent correspondence indicates that there were still problems with the lakes, with recent heavy rain necessitating repairs to the banks by the pagoda, and concerns being voiced over the water quality in the bathing lake – an issue that was to recur repeatedly. Bathing was considered important to the promotion of cleanliness and the prevention of disease, so the issue was taken seriously. Gibson investigated the problem with Mr Wicksteed, the East London Waterworks engineer. They found that the present water supply lay too near the outlet, resulting in an area of stagnant water, even though 60 gallons per minute were flushed through the pool. The proposed solution was to relocate the supply and provide additional inlets, ensuring an increased current.

It seems that Pennethorne was asked about the imperfect state of the walks and drives, which provided him with an opportunity to vent his feelings about Curtis. He said that much of the drive only had one coat of rough gravel as a foundation and no surface dressing, but that despite his remonstrations, Curtis would not follow his instructions, instead insisting that he was right. Pennethorne said that he overlooked Curtis's insults as he did not wish to disturb an arrangement made by the Board. It seems that the Board had taken to consulting Curtis independently, resulting in divided authority, which gave Curtis the grounds for acting as he did and undertaking 'to do everything by daywork cheaper and better than by contract'. Pennethorne's account indicates that some of the problems that beset the park during its establishment lay with the Board's arrangements and the underlying stress on financial control and expediency. Gibson set about addressing the problems, his efforts recognised by Edward Kemp in his account of the park, published in 1851:

> The site is in no way an inviting one ... For even here, where everything has been done in the most imperfect manner ... but we are happy to observe that it has begun in earnest by Mr Gibson, who has now been appointed to the charge of the park two years.

Whatever the park's inadequacies, people were using the space in growing numbers. Increasing use and an increase in the local population presented Gibson with a series of requests; first for an archery ground, which was sited in the south-eastern corner of the park, and then for permission to play trap ball on the ground used by the Victoria Park and Albert Cricket Clubs. The keeper was instructed to direct other sports to adjacent ground, to prevent damage to the cricket grounds, and Gibson produced a sketch of proposed arrangements to accommodate the various parties, which included 'many schools who frequent the park for practice of cricket and other games'.

A petition for occasional band performances resulted in the Royal Marine Band from Woolwich being engaged to play twice a week. Gibson selected the pagoda as the performance venue (there being no bandstand until 1865). Other petitions and memorials received during Gibson's tenure mostly requested new entrances, upon which both Pennethorne and Gibson were asked to comment, with their observations highlighting the need for new paths, planting and designated building land.

Many of Gibson's recommendations seem to have been implemented over the next few years, with work to the ornamental lake being undertaken in the winter of 1854–5. By 1857 Victoria Park had a head gardener, William Prestoe, and a carter, gardeners, labourers, constables, gate keepers and watchmen. Some of the staff lived in old cottages within the north boundary of the park and Gibson, as superintendent, resided in the principal lodge at Bonner Gate.

Although Pennethorne remained involved with the approaches to Victoria Park and its associated building development, once the park was established his services were in demand elsewhere, particularly at Battersea Park. By 1857, work was proceeding at Battersea and in 1858 Gibson left Victoria Park to supervise the levelling and planting there, a post secured for him by Pennethorne – Gibson must have won Pennethorne's confidence for the way he handled the challenges of Victoria Park. Battersea Park was to prove to be a significant challenge for both Pennethorne and Gibson. Pennethorne had full confidence in Gibson, saying he had 'always shown himself anxious to carry out my original intentions' and possessed 'such taste and knowledge as will enable him to carry out the Plan according to the instructions I shall give him respecting the levels, the choice of trees, &c. &c.' Within two months, and with rising costs, the work was brought to a halt because of a decision by Sir Benjamin Hall to cut off funds. Soon after taking office in 1855 he had begun a wide-ranging investigation into the management of the various Metropolitan Improvement schemes still being carried out by the Office of Works, telling Pennethorne to finish the park by August 1857, and not on any account to exceed the money voted by Parliament. Pennethorne refused to accept responsibility for the overspending and Hall relieved him of further control over the park in July 1857. He was replaced by John Gibson, who now had given up his responsibilities at Victoria Park. The remaining work on the park itself was eventually carried out with the aid of yet more money voted by Parliament. The work continued well into the 1860s, and, as a result of Gibson's careful management, the park was transformed into a varied and picturesque landscape with an exotic 'tropical garden', a grotto and profuse flower beds.

Bright-flowered tender annuals had dominated the bedding scene for about three decades when Gibson had decided to take a different approach. In 1864, he decided to experiment. Many new tender exotic plants had been arriving over the previous decades and what these lacked in bright flowers they more than made up for with striking foliage and form. Using such plants Gibson created new attractions – he studded an irregularly shaped lawn with tree ferns, planted eye-catching specimens such as palms, bananas, *Montanoa bipinnatifida* and *Wigandia caracasana*, as well as formal beds of *Solanum* and *Canna*. Thus, subtropical bedding was born. This style evolved with time as many of the tender subjects were replaced with hardy ones of similarly exotic form.

From its opening, the park was a tremendous success. Gibson's horticultural innovations were written up widely in the press. Day-trippers arriving by steamboat pushed the visitor numbers up to a reported 50,000 on a Sunday and Battersea Park became a place where people from all walks of life could come to spend their leisure hours, strolling around the paths, listening to the music, taking refreshment, boating on the lake or playing sport.

The successes of both Victoria Park and Battersea Park ensured further appointments for Gibson, and in 1871 he became superintendent of Hyde Park, St James's Park and Kensington Gardens. His final commission for a public park was for Cannon Hill Park, in Birmingham, which opened in 1873. The site on which Cannon Hill Park was developed in the late nineteenth century had previously been low-lying meadows associated with a

Sub-tropical garden in Battersea Park.

Gardeners at work in the sub-tropical garden in Battersea Park.

Promenading in Battersea Park.

Bedding displays at Cannon Hill Park, Birmingham.

Cannon Hill Park, Birmingham.

nineteenth-century villa, Cannon Hill House, which had been constructed on a knoll of high ground overlooking the valley of the River Rea. The Cannon Hill property formed part of the extensive Birmingham estates of Miss Louisa Ann Ryland of Barford Hill House, Warwickshire, the descendent of a prominent eighteenth-century Birmingham family. In April 1873 Miss Ryland presented some 57 acres at Cannon Hill to the Corporation; she also paid for the draining of the site, and its laying out and planting as a public park – based on the designs of John Gibson. His work was commended, as Gibson had taken advantage of all the natural characteristics of the ground, including its undulating nature and old trees, and 'supplemented them in the best possible taste with work that is at once novel and consistent with them'. The park's charming appearance was enhanced by rivulets, and newly planted shrubberies, flower beds, well-kept lawns and pools.

Cannon Hill Park was opened to the public on 1 September 1873 without public ceremony. In 1877, an anonymous visitor commented that the park was 'very pretty; laid out like Battersea Park'.

John Gibson died in 1875, leaving behind a legacy of three of the most significant parks of the Victorian era, which are as important today as they were when they were first laid out by one of the country's greatest plant collectors, park managers and park designers.

Edward Kemp (1817–1891)

Yet another protégé of Joseph Paxton, Edward Kemp was born in Streatham, Surrey. Very little is actually known about the young Edward Kemp's upbringing, education or the early part of his career. By the 1830s, he was working with Edward

Milner as a garden apprentice at Chatsworth House in Derbyshire, working under Joseph Paxton. By 1841, Kemp was living back in Streatham, with his occupation in the census of that year described as 'gardener'. He was certainly heavily involved at that time with botanical and gardening publications with Paxton, including *The Gardening Magazine*.

In August 1843, the Birkenhead Improvement Commissioners appointed Paxton to plan and construct what became Birkenhead Park, one of the first parks to have been provided in Britain at public expense. Edward Kemp was to play an important role, as Paxton appointed him to manage and direct the whole project. Progress was typically rapid, with plans being drawn up by Paxton, and, by the autumn, Paxton was asked to provide sketches for the seven lodges needed for the entrances and for the railings that surrounded the land. Kemp was given a permanent office and a monthly salary of £13 10s and, after some debate, a budget for materials including a spirit level and measuring tape. Soon there were hundreds of labourers excavating the lakes, setting drains and landscaping the park into mounds and sweeping contours. Paxton's plan for the park developed many of the ideas he had previously tested in Liverpool; in particular, the separation of different kinds of traffic and the opposition of open and intimate spaces. Groups of trees on raised mounds with luxuriant underplanting and pedestrian walks cutting across the expanse of the park were set against sinuous lakes with bridges and boathouses, a small rockery and narrower, winding paths. Formal bedding around the edges of the land was designed to link it to the proposed houses on the perimeter. From November that year to the following spring, Kemp was authorised to spend thousands of pounds on plants, including mature trees, tree-moving equipment and shrubs. None of Paxton's planting plans have survived, but Kemp, who was by now superintendent of the park, taking up this post in September 1843 when he was twenty-five, left a clear indication of the kinds of trees they used in a book he had published some years later. Underlining the importance of evergreens throughout the winter months, he recommended the use of evergreen oak, Scots fir, Austrian pine, cedar of Lebanon and Deodar cedar, as well as *Pinus excelsa* and the Douglas fir. These were mixed with the broader shapes of hardwoods and native trees, and exotic specimens were added for interest and individuality in order to provide a finely crafted tapestry of form, colour and texture.

By the summer of 1845, Paxton's work was more or less complete, with Kemp now retained as superintendent and to be provided with a residence. He was the first tenant of the Italian Lodge in Park Road South, but later lived at 74 Park Road West, where his monogram 'E. S. K.' may still be seen on the front chimney stack, along with the date 1859. The 'S' was the initial of his wife as, in September 1845, Kemp took leave of absence to marry Sophia, daughter of Henry Bailey, who had been park steward and gardener to the Spencer family at Althorp House. When Kemp returned to Birkenhead, his work did not fully occupy his time, and he became involved with planning a residential park estate, Carlett Park, at Eastham in the Wirral. The plans were not realised, and the commissioners were unhappy that Kemp had become involved in private practice. Birkenhead Park was opened officially in April 1847, and in 1849 the commissioners decided that a superintendent of parks was no longer required at Birkenhead. However, Kemp shrewdly negotiated a settlement that he should work here for no salary, but remain in his residence at the Italian Lodge plus be given a small plot of land for him to cultivate for his needs. The commissioners agreed, but Kemp clearly had to find other sources of income and went into private practice full time.

Like Edward Milner and his 'mentor', Joseph Paxton, Kemp was known for many private commissions. Kemp's clients were mainly the newly rich and wealthy, but he also gained commissions for the designs of some of the most significant parks and cemeteries in the country. These included Flaybrick Hill Cemetery in Birkenhead. Originally planned in the 1840s, Paxton had been approached to design a large municipal cemetery, but due to a recession and a subsequent decrease in the population, the plan went no further. By the 1860s, a boom in population made the provision of a new cemetery a priority once again. This time a competition was held for the design, which was won by none other than Kemp, who was assisted by Edward Mills, a prominent Birkenhead surveyor, and Messrs Lucy and Littler, architects of Liverpool. The cemetery was officially opened 30 May 1864 and named Birkenhead Cemetery.

Other commissions followed, which included Grosvenor Park in Chester. In 1867, the 2nd Marquis of Westminster, an extensive landowner in and around the city of Chester, commissioned Kemp and the Chester architect John Douglas to lay out a public park on a site, which was purchased at his behest, to the east of St John's Church in the centre of Chester. The Marquis of Westminster wrote to the city corporation on 5 October 1867 indicating his intention to place the new park 'in the hands of the Corporation as a gift on my part to the Citizens of Chester hoping it may afford health and recreation to themselves and their Families for many years to come'.

One of Kemp's earliest public commissions was in nearby Liverpool, becoming Newsham Park, which opened in 1868. Minutes from the Liverpool Finance Committee confirm that Edward Kemp, as a 'prominent local landscape architect and then incumbent park superintendent of Birkenhead Park', had been appointed to prepare the original draft design for Newsham Park. Kemp's initial plan and a transcript of his design comments was presented to the Borough Finance Committee on 25 November 1864. Furthermore, after this committee had referred Kemp's 'preliminary sketch' for consideration to the Borough Surveyor (Mr Weightman) and Architect (Mr Robson), Kemp had to revise his plan. The amended design was reported to the Committee on 16 December 1864, with the revision being largely driven by financial considerations and a desire to limit construction costs. The Committee resolved to approve Kemp's revised the plan on the recommendation of Robson, who commented that 'the arrangements now proposed are probably as good as any that could be devised'. Finally, on 2 March 1865, the Finance Committee resolved to approve the works, which had been estimated to total between £28,000 and £30,000. Although the park was subsequently enhanced and embellished with additional features, such as the bandstand and ornamental fountains, there is no doubt that the overall design intent and layout were Kemp's, and were a brave step for the young landscape designer.

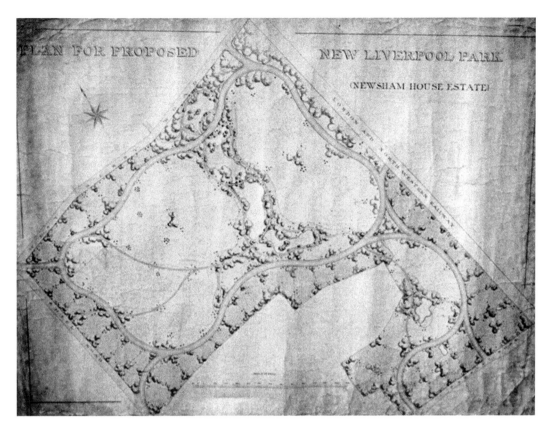

PLAN FOR PROPOSED NEW LIVERPOOL PARK

(NEWSHAM HOUSE ESTATE)

Kemp's plan for Newsham Park, Liverpool.

The park was intended to provide the inhabitants of this part of the city with an extensive open area for exercise, leisure and entertainment. The western side of the park received minimal planting and was left as largely open ground for games and walks. However, to the east an intricate and intimate landscape was created. Described in a twentieth-century guidebook 'as a placed oasis of wood and water amid dusty highways' (1934), it provided terrain for both passive enjoyment and active pursuits. Entirely man-made, this naturalistic section of the park included two lakes, which were designed for different purposes. A central component of Kemp's original design was a grand boulevard, punctuated by a series of elaborate and expensive fountains. The funding crisis temporarily halted the realisation of this plan and, when the park officially opened, it was without these ambitious and decorative features. Over the following thirty years building plots were gradually sold off, releasing funds for the park. In 1899 a smart, tree-lined boulevard, Garner's Drive, finally opened, leading from Prescot Drive to Sheil Road. A year later, four fountains were installed along its route. Although three of them were simple drinking fountains, the fourth was to become the jewel in the boulevard scheme. The Della Rabbia fountain was designed in the Italian style and named after a family of Italian Renaissance sculptors. Its dramatic arrangement of horses seated on a faux rockery proved a popular spectacle. Although

Hesketh Park bedding displays, Southport.

The floral clock in Hesketh Park, Southport.

Newsham officially opened in 1868, the lodges and gates were not in place until 1871. Nevertheless, whatever problems challenged the designers, the horticultural displays in Newsham were widely celebrated.

Hesketh Park in Southport was another commission, although some doubt exists as to how much involvement Paxton actually had here. Kemp was certainly involved, although may have simply been working to Paxton's plans. A public park was nevertheless created by the Southport Commissioners through the Second Southport Improvement Act of 1865 on 23 hectares of land donated by the Rev. Charles Hesketh. Kemp certainly laid out the park, with the cost of the layout being at £12,000 and the park eventually opening in 1868.

Stanley Park, Liverpool, was another commission, following on from his work at Newsham Park. It was designed by Kemp in 1867 and was laid out in 1867–70. It was named after Lord Stanley of Preston, a former Lord Mayor of Liverpool. The park's original architectural features were designed by the corporation surveyor E. R. Robson (1835–1917) and the total cost, including the purchase of the land and the costs of the architectural features, was £154,398. Plots of land to the south of the park were sold off for housing in order to fund the project. The opening of the park in May 1870 attracted 25–30,000 people and was recorded in the *Illustrated London News*.

The Grade II listed Gladstone Conservatory in Stanley Park was first built in 1870 at a cost of £12,000. It was originally intended to house the tropical and exotic plants being grown in the surrounding greenhouses.

Kemp's reputation was spreading. In 1856, Congleton Town Council bought 12 acres of land between Town Wood and the River Dane with the object of creating an open space in which to lay out a public park. A park committee was appointed but they seemingly needed reassurance about the site. One advisor to whom they applied was James Bateman, who had developed a series of impressive gardens at Biddulph Grange. The *Congleton and Macclesfield Mercury* reported on 27 October 1860: 'We understand that James Bateman, Esq., The Grange, has in the company with other members of the Park Committee declared the spot admirably suited to the purpose contemplated' – i.e. a public park. As parks were a matter of public pride, their design was as important as that of public buildings, which were built on a grand scale with meticulous attention to detail. Just as a notable architect was employed to design buildings, so too were the equivalent landscape designers and gardeners employed for the parks. The designer eventually appointed to Congleton Park was Edward Kemp, who was helped by the Congleton surveyor William Blackshaw. In Congleton Park, Paxton's principles are particularly noticeable in the carriageway running around the outside of the park and in its proximity to the river. Paxton always emphasised water features; he also encouraged the creation of formal gardens and pathways running through them and areas 'for the passive enjoyment of the park's scenery'. Kemp provided these features as well as seating and viewing points in the park and in the Town Wood. Adhering to Paxton's designs he also allowed a large amount of open space surrounded by trees. In time, other characteristics came to be added, including a bowling green and a croquet lawn, with provisions for boating being made. In addition, he created a network of winding paths through the wood, many of which were designed to create unexpected twists and views. The paths in Town Wood culminated in a high view point, which later became the site for the Russian cannon. Congleton Park was finally opened in 1871.

One of Kemp's grandest public park designs, however, would be much further afield, and would be what became known as Saltwell Park in Gateshead. The town, for much of the nineteenth century, was not a pleasant place to live in, with the growing population being crammed into tenements on Gateshead's quayside and in ramshackle courts and entries running off Bottle Bank and the High Street. One of Gateshead's leading industrialists was William Wailes, one of the country's principal stained glass window manufacturers, who, in 1853, had purchased the bulk of an area known as the Saltwell Cottage Estate. Wailes never had any intention of selling his estate to a speculative builder. Instead, he sold his land and everything on it, including his house, to Gateshead Corporation as a public park. After considerable debate in the Council Committee, a letter appeared in the *Gateshead Observer* on 10 October 1874, urging the council to buy Wailes' estate as it was suggested that his land might be suitable, seeing that 'his grounds ... were laid out by one of the most eminent landscape gardeners in the country'. This was none other than Edward Kemp. Wailes had played a major part in creating Saltwell Towers and the grounds, with Kemp engaged in laying out his grounds. In fact, Kemp had written in his book on garden design, published in 1858: 'Saltwell near Gateshead, where regular oblong beds were cut out in a band of grass on either side of the walk... The walk itself, along the front of the kitchen garden ... was entered through a wire arch mantled with climbing roses'.

Kemp's involvement in the design of the public park was initially stalled though, as Gateshead Council asked John Hancock, the noted Newcastle naturalist, to provide a design. He declined and it was Wailes who suggested that Kemp be employed to lay out the new park, who charged four guineas per day plus travelling expenses. Kemp presented his first plan to the council on 3 February 1876. His estimates for laying out the park were also submitted with the final figure excluding any buildings and came to £10,862 19s 9d.

The park opened to the public in May 1876, with Kemp's planned features still on paper. His challenge was to design a landscape for the whole of the park and include such features as new paths and walkways that would lead people to explore the whole estate in a comfortable and uncrowded atmosphere. He had 52 acres in which to do this. Kemp's second set of plans were displayed at the Town Hall in July 1876 and it was not long before there was pressure to start work on them. His ideas included widening the existing footpaths, creating a promenade walk and designing a main entrance at the north-east corner of the park – a sensible idea, as it was close to where new housing was being planned. It also provided the visitor with a staggering panoramic view across the park, giving the illusion of vast swathes of greenery. Kemp also provided for a bowling green, a skating rink, a croquet lawn, a lake of about three acres, a refreshment room and a site for a drinking fountain. Although most of Kemp's ideas were adopted, the debate on iron railings around the park continued as the Parks Committee discussed this over a lengthy

PROMENADE, SALTWELL PARK, GATESHEAD.

Saltwell Park, Gateshead, and Kemp's promenade.

The main drive and lodge, Queen's Park, Crewe.

Queen's Park, Crewe.

Hesketh Park, Southport.

period of time. Many considered it an extravagance. Eventually, a mix of iron and wooden railings were added to the park. The council were determined to ensure that all of Kemp's features were added and with many further applications to the Board of Health, most were successful, along with the additions of two shelter houses, the lake, a children's playground and a gymnasium. A refreshment house, further entrance gates and three lodges, together with extra provision of drainage and a second storey to the park superintendent's house were all provided. By 1889, the park was deemed 'a great boon to the population after work hours'.

Queen's Park in Crewe was Kemp's final park design, opening in 1888. It was designed in conjunction with F. W. Webb, the chief mechanical engineer of the London & North Western Railway, at a cost of £10,000, and retains many of their original features to this day.

The importance of Edward Kemp's work cannot be underestimated. His earliest impact on Birkenhead Park is clearly recognised but unlike Milner and Gibson, Paxton's other protégés, Kemp's output in relation to public parks was much greater, and none more so than in the north-west of England. His influence on other garden designers, including Thomas H. Mawson, who went on to design Hanley Park and Burslem Park in Stoke-on Trent, is also recognised today. Edward Kemp died at his home in Birkenhead Park in 1891 and he was buried in Flaybrick Cemetery, Birkenhead.

Edward Milner (1819–1884)

Edward Milner was born on 20 January 1819 in Darley Dale, Derbyshire, and was the eldest child of Henry and Mary Milner. His father was a sawyer who was employed on the Chatsworth estate in 1825 as a gardener – the estate of the Duke of Devonshire. In 1826, the Duke appointed Joseph Paxton to be the superintendent of the gardens at Chatsworth. This partnership would be one of the most significant episodes in national horticultural history, as described previously, and it was Paxton who inspired a further generation of gardeners. One of these was Henry Milner's son, Edward, who would become one of the most prominent landscape gardeners and park designers, with his legacy still omnipresent up until the twenty-first century.

   Milner caught Paxton's eye, who recognised his potential from a very early age. It was Paxton who enabled the young Edward Milner to attend the Lady Manners Grammar School in Bakewell, clearly aware of his own lack of formal education. Little is known of this arrangement, but Milner was soon to become Paxton's apprentice, in around the time of Paxton's conversion of the Duke's greenhouse into a modern stove. Paxton was to have a significant impact on Edward Milner's career from the outset. The commissions he received were to frequently give rise to major opportunities for Edward. In 1838, Paxton was given his first public appointment when he, Dr John Lindley (a professor of botany at University College, London) and the Earl of Surrey's head gardener were asked to inspect and report on the royal gardens. After the death of George II and Sir Joseph Banks in 1820, the gardens, including Kew Gardens, had been badly neglected and had been allowed to

Edward Milner.

decline. With Queen Victoria now on the throne, an investigation of royal management and expenditure was set up and the trio's report recommended a complete reformation of the system, leading specifically to Kew Gardens becoming public property. Milner was to become significantly involved as a result of these recommendations. In December 1840, Edward Milner, almost twenty-two years of age, took the train to London to visit various horticultural establishments, including J. & C. Lee's Nursery in Hammersmith, describing its condition as being in 'the most deplorable state'. He went on to the Horticultural Society's garden in Chiswick, where he was impressed with what he saw. His trip continued and included Kew, where his comments were mixed; he was impressed with the New Conservatory built by William IV but less so with the Palm House, which he felt was too small for the 'very fine specimens' within. His journey took in other gardens before he returned to Derbyshire for Christmas. Paxton was sufficiently impressed with the results of Edward's report of his London visit that he was sent to Paris to study at the Jardins des Plantes, France's principal botanic garden, for four years.

His time in Paris was well used and the knowledge he gained significant. He visited many gardens for Dr John Lindley, the editor of *The Gardener's Chronicle*. This weekly journal, which has been considered to be the greatest revolution in horticultural publishing, was started by Lindley and Paxton in 1840. Milner's first impact on the growing park movement was as a direct result of Paxton. Paxton himself had been involved with Prince's Park in Liverpool since 1842. Prince's Park was designed by Paxton and was his first independent work on a park. The design was influenced by Regents Park, and it was the first in a sequence of parks by Paxton and his followers that were to be enormously influential on the design of public parks thereafter. Joseph Paxton was commissioned to design the Prince's Park together with the surrounding belt of housing by Richard Vaughan Yates in 1842. The rent from the building plots was designed to pay for the maintenance of the park, which was exclusively for the use of residents. Following Yates' death, the reversionary interest in the land was conveyed to Liverpool Corporation in 1884 and, after protracted negotiations with the Yates family, Liverpool Corporation took over the park in 1918. Paxton appointed Edward as park superintendent to oversee the landscaping during his absence. His notebook contains a list of seeds that were sown in Prince's Park and his involvement was to last until 1846. Further commissions of Paxton were to result in a growing workload for Milner, including work at Tatton Park near Knutsford and London Road Cemetery in Coventry.

Paxton's greatest achievement was, without a doubt, the Great Exhibition of 1851. The extent of Milner's involvement in this is not known, but one has to assume he was associated with it in some way. With the closure of the exhibition in October and the formation of the Crystal Palace Company in May 1852, the decision was taken to move it bit by bit to Penge Park in Sydenham. Fox and Henderson, the original contractors, dismantled the huge structure and transported it piece by piece by horse and cart. Edward was appointed Superintendent of Works, and was responsible for the grounds at Sydenham. His impact and involvement was considerable.

As the new Crystal Palace was being erected, Edward was responsible for much of the landscape works, laying out the Italian terraces, and the raised Rosary and English landscape garden, but to Paxton's design. Two large and impressive water towers, with reservoirs and ten miles of piping were required to feed the nearly 12,000 jets. The largest of the fountains were designed to project jets 280 feet above the vast basins. At the lower end of the park was the tidal lake, where Edward had employed Paxton's idea from Birkenhead Park insomuch that the full extent of the lake could not be viewed in its entirety, giving the impression of a greater size. On 10 June 1854, the park was opened by Queen Victoria in the presence of over 40,000 people, with both Paxton and Milner present. The new Crystal Palace Park, under Milner, was characterised for plantings in geometric patterns and the use of primary colours, which was favoured by Owen Jones, who was responsible for much of the Palace's interior. Edward had made much use of yellow and scarlet combinations and blues with purples. The planting of countless thousands of seedlings and the other ground work involved was an immense piece of work and by May 1855, Edward was overseeing the work of about 450 gardeners. However, by this time, Edward was now turning his attention to another park project with Paxton – on this occasion, in the Pennine Hills of West Yorkshire.

Together with Paxton's son-in-law, the architect George Stokes, they laid out the site of the People's Park in Halifax for the industrialist and carpet manufacturer Sir Francis Crossley, Member of Parliament for the town. Crossley had visited the USA in 1855, where he had been inspired by the White Mountains and had resolved on his return that both nature and art should be available to the people of Halifax. Paxton's design drew upon that of the Crystal Palace, in the use of the axial principle with mounds and a small lake. It was Edward Milner who was given the task of supervising the works which included huge quantities of topsoil that were brought in and the laying out of winding

Paxton's upper terrace at People's Park, Halifax.

paths, the trees, shrubs, flower beds, rockeries and a lake, while Stokes designed the pavilion. People's Park was opened in August 1857 at a cost of £50,000, by which time Paxton, Milner and Stokes had moved on to their next project for the Scarborough Cliff Bridge Company, a project that involved a new pavilion, linked colonnade, music hall and a bandstand.

Changes were afoot at Chatsworth though, with the death of the 6th Duke of Devonshire in January 1858, and both Paxton and Milner broke with the estate. It was the catalyst for change, particularly for Edward Milner. He was living close to the Crystal Palace and had made many connections and gained a number of his own private commissions. Yet, having learnt from Paxton that public works were far more profitable and financially rewarding, he endeavoured to gain such commissions himself as an independent practice, the first being the laying out of Stoney Royd Cemetery in Halifax, which he won in April 1860 and which opened in 1861. This led to further work and he was to become gainfully engaged in three parks in Preston, namely Avenham, Miller and Moor Parks. As the American Civil War interrupted the supply of cotton to the Lancashire cotton industry, Alderman Thomas Miller, the proprietor of Horrockses, Miller & Co., bequeathed land for the first two parks from his Avenham estate, which was situated to the south-west of Preston. Miller managed to keep some of his employees in work by redirecting their labour to the construction of the parks and by paying them out of his own pocket to prevent them from having to survive from poor relief. Edward's designs for the 26-acre Avenham Park and the 11-acre Miller Park were supervised by George

Belvedere, Avenham Park, Preston.

Rowbotham, who continued with the parks after their construction as the park-keeper. Pulhams were employed for the implementation of the rockwork.

The two parks were adjacent to each other but were divided by an embankment of the East Lancashire Railway. For Miller Park, Edward had designed a terrace walk, which was decorated with large vases and a central staircase leading down to a circular pool with a fountain. At the higher end, Edward placed a stone belvedere and both parks were planted with numerous trees and shrubs. Costing £20,200, the two parks were opened on 3 October 1867 by the Duke of Cambridge, along with Preston Town Hall. Moor Park had been open since 1833 and was 100 acres in extent. Edward retained all the features of the original plan but made a number of additions, including roads, trees, shrubs, a rock garden and a cricket ground, all at a cost of £10,800. It was reopened the day after the smaller parks.

Edward was less successful in his endeavours when it came to the competition for the award for the laying out of Sefton Park in Liverpool in 1867. Lying to the south-east and almost adjoining the site of his first work at Prince's Park, this must have been especially disappointing to Edward. It was at about this time, however, that Edward's eldest son, Henry Ernest, joined his practice. Henry had been sent to France and Germany to be educated by private tutors, with formal training in architecture and engineering. By 1871 Henry had been elected an associate of the Institution of Civil Engineers as he was about to enter partnership with his father.

Edward was about to commence one of the most important public park commissions of his career. He had gained the contract for the Arboretum in Lincoln on the basis of his reputation as 'the eminent landscape gardener from the Crystal Palace Company', as well as for his work at Hartsholme Hall. It was to be one of Henry and Edward's first jobs together. In 1868, fields lying to the south-west of Lincoln Cathedral were proposed as a site for the Arboretum and Edward was asked to report on its suitability, and to propose a design for the site. Unfortunately, the Corporation failed to secure the land and the project stalled as an alternative site was looked for. In 1870, Monks Leys Common was purchased by the Corporation and, in July, Edward was once again asked to inspect the site and develop a new plan. Considering the topographical similarities of the two sites, it was not surprising that Edward's 'new' proposals were described by one of the Arboretum Committee members as being 'somewhat similar to the previous one'. Nevertheless, Edward's design was approved on 13 September 1870. Edward commenced the detailed designs almost immediately, including the entrance gates, the West Gate Lodge and Refreshment Room (to accommodate 200 people), a serpentine lake crossed by two bridges, a maze of briar bushes and a glass pavilion flanked by fountains running east to west on a terrace on the steeply sloping site.

The project was not without its problems though. Despite trial holes being sunk to ascertain the nature of the ground, its waterlogged condition and liability to slide were only discovered once the terrace and retaining wall had been built. With a collapse of the wall due to a landslip, Edward insisted that deep draining had revealed that the problem had originated 15 feet below its foundation. Edward was of the view that this could not have been foreseen but the Committee did not agree and held Edward professionally

Bedding displays in Miller Park, Preston.

Derby Promenade, Miller Park, Preston.

Derby Promenade, Miller Park, Preston.

71

The Swings on Moor Park, Preston.

Moor Park, Preston, and children at play.

responsible for not predicting the landslides. The extra work and the delays pushed the cost of the project above £8,000, which was almost twice the initial estimate.

The Arboretum opened on 26 August 1872 with 25,000 people attending, to be entertained by brass band concerts, performing dogs, the Midland Aeronaut in his new balloon and the fireworks by Mr Wells of Crystal Palace. The bitterness continued between Edward and the Committee, who refused to pay his outstanding bill of £289 and 'acidic' correspondence was regularly exchanged. Sadly, there were other wall failures, which further undermined Edward's position, so in 1877 he finally accepted a reduced payment of £105.

Despite such animosity, it was not Milner's last involvement with the Arboretum. From 1883, the owner of Hartsholme Hall was Nathaniel Clayton Cockburn, a grandson of Nathaniel Clayton, who had been Joseph Shuttleworth's professional partner. Clayton owned an acre of land adjoining the north-west of the Arboretum, which had been purchased to prevent the building of houses that could overlook his mansion and grounds. After his grandfather's death, Cockburn presented the land to the Corporation and it was laid out by none other than Henry Milner during 1894–95. Henry arranged the paths on the extremely steep site, on to which he transplanted mature trees from the old part of the Arboretum. The cost of this work was about £1,000 and it was opened as the Arboretum's north-west extension in August 1895.

Another public commission that Edward was awarded was the contract for laying out the Pavilion Gardens in Buxton. He was certainly well placed to gain this with his early connections with Chatsworth, Paxton and the Crystal Palace. Paxton had previously been involved in earlier investments in the town made by the 6th Duke of Devonshire, which

Lincoln Arboretum.

included a park. The 7th Duke of Devonshire gave the Buxton Improvements Company 12 acres of land and it was Edward Milner who was commissioned to lay out a new park. Work began in August 1870 as Edward dammed the River Wye to create cascades and waterfalls and designed a footbridge to link the Dutch Garden, rose mount and bandstand to a 400-foot-long iron and glass pavilion. The pavilion, which comprised a domed central hall flanked by conservatories, was lit by gas and heated by hot water pipes to allow the locals to enjoy garden strolls while protected from the severest of Peak District winters. It certainly resembled a smaller Crystal Palace, particularly in the detail of the window decoration. Edward added a number of local touches such as a row of ducal coronets on the roof and stag's heads, from the Cavendish coat of arms, in the interior ironwork. There were complaints from some locals who were unhappy about the imposition of an entrance fee. The Pavilion Gardens were opened by the Duke of Devonshire on 10 August 1871 with a public luncheon held in the Pavilion. Further private work was to follow and kept Edward and Henry gainfully occupied, including for the Chamberlains of Birmingham.

Further public commissions were few and far between, but did include a number of improvements at Royal Victoria Park in Bath. It had opened in 1830 and was now in need of renovation. Edward made the existing oval pond shallower and increased its size by using Paxton's method of convoluting the shape to give the impression of even greater size. A small island and promontory were formed, the latter being the site of the Victoria Vase, which marked the fiftieth anniversary of the park's opening in 1880.

St Paul's Cathedral in London is another of Edward's most identifiable commissions. In 1878, the agreement of the Dean and Chapter instigated the creation of four

The Pavilion, Buxton.

Pavilion Gardens, Buxton.

recreational gardens at the north-west, north-east, south-west and south-east points of the compass around St Paul's. Edward laid out all four gardens for a fee of £5,000 but only his plan for the north-west garden appears to have survived. The gardens were opened by the Lord Mayor on 22 September 1879.

By now, Edward's health had deteriorated. He had been nominated for fellowship of the Linnean Society in 1881 and had contributed to the laying out of Hartshill Cemetery in Stoke-on-Trent. Edward was to die at his home, Hillside, in Norwood, on 26 March 1884 at the age of sixty-five, and he was buried at St Helen's Church in Darley Dale, Derbyshire. He received glowing tributes in *The Garden* and *The Gardener's Chronicle*. His work was to continue through his son Henry and a fitting tribute to his father was his book *The Art and Practice of Landscape Gardening*, which was published in 1890. Henry used the preface to highlight Edward's contribution to the profession, which is still recognised today, particularly with the public parks so many now enjoy. His contribution is especially significant due to being, along with Edward Kemp and John Gibson, one of Paxton's trio of protégés.

Alexander McKenzie (1829–1893)

Alexander McKenzie was born in 1829 in Auldearn, Nairnshire, Scotland. He starting out as a nurseryman in Brighton and worked as a landscape gardener and land surveyor, moving to London in 1851 where he worked at the Royal Botanical Gardens and on land belonging to the King of Belgium. By 1863, he had been appointed as superintendent of Alexandra Palace and Park, which he laid out with a pattern of informal walks leading down through lawns set with specimen trees, shrubs and informal bedding. He then became the superintendent of open spaces owned by the Metropolitan Board of Works, giving him responsibility for Finsbury Park, Southwark Park, Victoria Embankment, Albert Embankment, Hampstead Heath, Blackheath, Shepherd's Bush, Stepney Green, Hackney Commons and London Fields. He also took on private landscape design work in England, Ireland and Scotland, including work for the directors of the Metropolitan and City Police orphanage, the board of management of the Middlesex County Asylum, Birmingham Town Council and the Lord Provost, magistrates and council of the city of Edinburgh. From 1879 Alexander McKenzie was employed as superintendent of Epping Forest and remained in this post until his death in April 1893, when he was succeeded as superintendent by his son, Frank Fuller McKenzie.

McKenzie also contributed to gardening magazines, and was the author of *The Parks, Open Spaces and Thoroughfares of London*, which was published 1869. In this he wrote, 'For some years past I have devoted much attention to the best modes of improving the British Metropolis, with a view first, to the health of its dense population, and next, in order to render it somewhat more worthy of comparison with France than it is at present...'

McKenzie described the public parks as the 'lungs of the metropolis', with more than 2,000 acres of 'park proper' in London itself. McKenzie was not keen on extensive floral displays nor on sub-tropical gardens, believing them to be extravagant and too expensive, and that they should be limited to certain areas only.

McKenzie's influence on many of London's parks was considerable, and none more so than with Finsbury Park. The park was created under the auspices of the Metropolitan Board of Works following the Finsbury Park Act of Parliament of 1857 in order to provide a much-needed municipal park for Finsbury residents, whereby it became London's second municipal park after Victoria Park. Although the Act had specified that 250 acres of parkland should be retained free of development, when work finally began in 1866 it was reduced to an area of 115 acres, purchased at £472 per acre. Discussions around creating a park here had arisen prior to the Act when a plan for what was proposed as Albert Park had been drawn up in the early 1850s by James Pennethorne, the designer of Victoria Park in Hackney and Battersea Park. The structure of the park, including its five entrance gates and the Lodge at Manor Gate, as well as the perimeter carriage drive and the main paths, was designed by Frederick Manable, superintending architect to the Metropolitan Board of Works. Various areas of formal planting were set within open parkland as the 'ornamental portion of the park', which included the American Gardens and a network of curving paths within the perimeter drive, all of which was designed by McKenzie himself, who was now the Board's landscape designer.

As landscape designer for the Metropolitan Board of Works, his impact at Southwark Park is also to be recognised as he was responsible for laying out the park. Prior to becoming a public park, the site was used for market gardening and was owned by the Lord of Rotherhithe Manor. Pressure for a public park in the area began in the 1850s, and in 1857 the new Metropolitan Board of Works was persuaded that Bermondsey and Rotherhithe, as well as Finsbury, were most in need and a site was approved. Southwark

Finsbury Park and flowerbeds.

Boating lake in Finsbury Park.

The lake, Southwark Park.

Park was laid out by McKenzie and opened on 19 June 1869. The original layout had a wide carriage drive around the perimeter, part of which survives; various facilities were added by 1885, including a new lake and a bandstand.

Thomas Hayton Mawson (1861–1933)

Thomas Hayton Mawson was a landscape architect, and was born on 5 May 1861 in Nether Wyersdale, Lancashire. He was educated at the local church school, and then at the age of twelve joined a builder's business in Lancaster. Two years later he returned home to help his father set up a nursery, but the venture failed and the family eventually moved to London, where Thomas secured work with John Wills, a well-known floral decorator. In 1881, he took a job at Hale Farm Nurseries; not long afterwards, he accepted a partnership with a firm of contractors in order to start experimenting with his ideas on design. When this fell through too, he decided to set up a family business and, with his two brothers, established a nursery and contracting firm in Windermere. From designing local private gardens, the firm progressed to contracts from all parts of the country, which eventually included the design of many public parks and a number of

Thomas H. Mawson.

town planning schemes. On 1 August 1884, Mawson married Anna, a nurse, daughter of Edward Prentice, a surgeon, of North Walsham. They had four sons and five daughters. The eldest son, Edward Prentice Mawson, became a successful landscape architect in his own right, and eventually took over the running of his father's firm.

By 1900 Thomas Mawson had left Mawson Brothers to pursue a separate career in landscape design. He achieved great success and became the leading landscape architect of the day, completing over 200 garden commissions in England, Scotland and Wales, with formal designs near to the house and informal layouts leading towards the surrounding countryside. His public works were numerous and included Belle Vue Park, Newport (1894); Burslem Park, Stoke-on-Trent (1894); East Park, Wolverhampton (1896); Hanley Park, Stoke-on-Trent (1897); Broomfield Park, Enfield (1903); Falinge Park, Rochdale (1906); Barrow Public Park, Barrow-in-Furness (1908); Haslam Park, Preston (1910); Stanley Park, Blackpool (1926); and Vale Park, Aylesbury (1933). His impact on the design of public parks was considerable, with an output rarely achieved by many of his contemporaries.

The land on which Belle Vue Park stands was a gift to Newport from Godfrey Morgan, 1st Viscount Tredegar, in 1891, to provide a public park for its citizens. An open competition to design and construct the park was won by Mawson. His winning design was, in fact, designed for the neighbouring field – the site of the then Newport & Monmouthshire Hospital, after Mawson misunderstood directions on his first visit to Newport. The mistake wasn't realised until the first site visit, after the contract had been awarded, and Mawson had to quickly re-think some of his plans. Belle Vue Park was, in fact, Thomas Mawson's first win in an open competition. In November 1892, Lord Tredegar performed the ceremony of cutting the first sod; construction began and the park opened on 8 September 1894, with the final cost of the park at £19,500. Belle Vue Park has many features typical of a Victorian public park and it is certainly typical of a Thomas Mawson design, when one considers his other work at Burslem Park and Hanley Park in particular, both in Stoke-on-Trent. It includes conservatories and a pavilion, as well as a bandstand on a rather grandiose terrace, along with a number of rockeries within the park. Additional features were also added to the park throughout the years.

Burslem Park was also a typical Mawson design. He had become renowned for the creation of landscapes that utilised his architectural and horticultural skills and emphasised a strong association between built form and the immediate landscape. His approach to landscape design of estate land typically included a formal terrace adjacent to the main house, with ornamental lawns and herbaceous borders, sometimes at lower levels, and more informal circuitous paths, shrub beds and tree planting to link with farmland or the natural landscape beyond. Signature features often found in Mawson gardens and parks included timber pergolas with stone pillars, sweeping steps and stylish seats, gates, fences and garden ornaments. This was certainly apparent in his design for Burslem Park. It consisted of a number of features, including the two shelters on the terrace and another shelter erected above the lake on a reclaimed pit mound. Two terracotta fountains were erected on either side of the bandstand on the terrace. The park gates and seats were donated by the manufacturers, while the main gates near the

Thomas Mawson's amended design for Haslam Park, 1912. (© Preston Digital Archive)

Moorland entrance were made by Messrs Brown of Birmingham, but were designed by Mawson himself. However, the focus of the park is the pavilion, in the fashionable late nineteenth-century Elizabethan style, which stands on the eastern edge of the terrace. Situated towards the eastern boundary of the site is a levelled platform (used before 1893 as an athletics ground), which is laid out as a formal flower garden that is separated by paths into eight level grass areas, each with central perennial planting borders. To the east of the pavilion is a second formal garden, again laid out on a level platform, which would seem to be a later modification of Mawson's original design – one bowling green and a recreation space with the associated restored shrubbery planting.

At East Park, Wolverhampton, the council's Borough Surveyor advertised for designs for a new park to be built, with seventeen submissions entered. Mawson's was the winning design. In October 1893, the costs were estimated at £6,000, which was double the original amount anticipated. Mawson's final plan for East Park was slightly altered but work was to begin in earnest in 1893, with Mawson regularly attending consultancy meetings with the council. Mawson's design for East Park would include a central driveway, which led to a large lake and was overshadowed by small wooded hills. On the

Park gates, Burslem Park, Stoke-on-Trent.

far side of the park, known as Stow Heath, there were raised hills that were used as a viewing platform. Visitors would be able to look at the boating activity on the lake and view further on into the park. Circumventing the park were avenues of trees that had been planted on Mawson's suggestion, which acted as a screen to obscure the view of dereliction from the surrounding area and other works that were occurring at the time.

One of the many inter-war parks, Stanley Park, Blackpool, is of particular historical importance and is possibly the finest example of a municipal park of the 'Arts and Craft' style in the country. Stanley Park's importance stems from the quality of the original design by Mawson who had a great affinity for the Arts and Crafts Movement, which was in vogue in the 1920s, and the fact that the overall layout has changed little since its opening by Edward George Villiers Stanley in 1926 also adds to the importance of this park. Although some significant assets came later, such as the café building, (a fine example of the Arts and Crafts style of architecture) and Cocker Memorial Tower, which was built in the 1930s, these elements are regarded as integral features of the park and add to its overall heritage value. Mawson created a new vision for a park, which was developed and detailed in a document published in 1922 entitled 'Blackpool, The New Park and Recreation Ground'. Stanley Park was part of an overall radical vision of Blackpool Council in the period preceding the Second World War, which aimed to provide additional recreational land for a town that was rapidly becoming overdeveloped. Siting the park away from the coast was deliberate, with the aim to increase the variety of attractions in the town. Alderman Sir Lindsay Parkinson had acquired the site of two former brickworks and some agricultural land on the east side of Blackpool with

The Italian Gardens, Stanley Park, Blackpool.

the plan to develop a park already in mind. This land, together with donations of land from other dignitaries, made up the area that is the site of Stanley Park today. The land previously consisted of 'the most heterogeneous collection of hen runs, pigsties, stagnant ponds, caravan dwellings and stables we have ever come across. The buildings were of temporary nature, margarine boxes, tea chests, biscuit tins and petrol cans being pressed into service for walls and roofing material'.

The council had chosen well in appointing Thomas Mawson, and the scheme he provided demonstrated his abilities as a landscape architect with great affinity for the Arts and Crafts Movement. The park took four years to construct and, when opened in 1926, Mawson had left Blackpool with a heritage asset unsurpassed for its time, and which was probably the most significant municipal park of its day in the country.

Many of Mawson's parks included bandstands, which were becoming popular in public parks from the late nineteenth century, with many of them being made of cast iron from the foundries of Macfarlane, Smith and McDowall, Steven & Co. from Glasgow. Mawson was quoted in *Civic Art* in 1911 as saying:

> The provision of good music within the park is of almost greater importance than the provision of opportunities for physical recreation, for nothing gives more pleasure, and there is surely no more elevating or inspiring force... A cheap cast iron bandstand, and fine classical music played with that consummate skill for which many of our orchestral bands are famous, are anomalous. Apart from its use, the spider-like construction in chocolate, blue and gold, standing in its circle of red ashes or black asphalt, makes the whole park vulgar.

The bandstand, Stanley Park, Blackpool.

Mawson clearly recognised the value of 'good music within the park', but was no fan of the 'cheap cast iron bandstand'.

Mawson also published two main works, *The Art and Craft of Garden Making* (1900), which ran into five editions, and *Civic Art* (1911), in which he discussed the principles of town planning. From 1910 to 1924 he lectured regularly at the School of Civic Design, Liverpool University. Conscious that he lacked formal education, the need for education was among his lifelong concerns. Mawson was elected an honorary member of the Royal Institute of British Architects in 1903 and became a member of the Art Workers' Guild in 1905. He was made a freeman of the City of London in 1917 and an honorary liveryman of the Worshipful Company of Gardeners. In 1921, he became a fellow of the Linnean Society. In 1923, he was elected president of the Town Planning Institute and the following year he was appointed to the Royal Fine Arts Commission. In 1929, he became the first president of the Institute of Landscape Architects. From 1923, he suffered from Parkinson's disease, which caused his death at his home, Applegarth, Hest Bank, Lancashire, on 14 November 1933.

The Great Municipal Designers

William Wallace Pettigrew (1867–1947)

William Wallace Pettigrew was born at Dumfries House, Ayrshire, in 1867, and was eldest son of Head Gardener Andrew Pettigrew. He trained at the Royal Botanical Gardens, Kew, from 1888 to 1889. He then worked as a gardener at Dunkeld House, followed by Culzean Castle, before moving back to Cardiff to take on the role as Cardiff's first parks superintendent, working under William Harpur, the Borough Engineer. The Parks Committee decided that he should be 'Superintendent of the Public Parks & Open Spaces', whereupon he would report directly to the committee – a position that he held for more than twenty-three years. He lived at Roath Park House, the residence of the parks superintendent, with his wife, Ruth McConochie, whom he married in 1894. He also wrote the official *Guide to Roath Park and Catalogue of Plants in Botanical Garden*, which was published for the Cardiff Corporation by the *Western Mail* in 1905. Some of Pettigrew's monthly reports to the Parks Committee have survived in a handwritten book covering the period January 1908 to October 1912. Pettigrew worked tirelessly with William Harpur to create many of Cardiff's finest parks, including Roath Park, Victoria Park, Cathays Park, Llandaff Fields, Pontcanna Fields, Waterloo Gardens, Roath Mill Gardens and Roath Brook Gardens.

William Wallace Pettigrew.
(Courtesy of Tim Pettigrew)

In 1915, he moved to Manchester Corporation to take on the Chief Parks Officer role, where he perceived 'there was more scope' and his role in Cardiff was taken over by his youngest brother, Andrew Alexander Pettigrew. When Pettigrew resigned, the Parks Committee recorded its:

Appreciation of the conscientious, faithful and efficient manner in which he has at all times during a period of 23½ years, discharged, with complete satisfaction to this Committee and the Council, the important duties appertaining to this Office. While regretting to be deprived of the valuable services of so capable an officer, this Committee desire cordially to congratulate him on his important and well-merited appointment at Manchester and to tender to Mr Pettigrew their sincere and hearty good wishes for his future success in his new position.

Pettigrew's career in Manchester was equally notable. Holding the distinguished post of President of the Institute between 1926 and 1929, he also played a major part in the creation of the Institute of Park & Recreation Administration. During his working life, he was an ardent supporter of educating young gardeners in the public sector, and was always active in promoting parks and horticulture through lectures and written work. His tireless work led to the award of the Victoria Medal for Horticulture by the Royal Horticultural Society in 1927, and he was widely respected by his peers across the UK. He wrote *Commonsense Gardening* in 1925 and *Municipal Parks* in 1937.

Philips Park, Manchester.

William remained in Manchester until his retirement in 1932, when he moved to the Sussex coast, but four years later he was to return to Cardiff to take up his old post on a temporary basis after the sudden death of his brother from cancer in 1936.

When he retired in 1932, he and his wife Ruth moved to Eastbourne. In retirement, he wrote a definitive textbook on park management, which he dedicated to the memory of his brother Andrew. He and Ruth both died in Eastbourne in early 1947. An obituary published in the *Journal of Park Administration, Horticulture and Recreation* (reprinted in the *Kew Guild Journal*) stated that while at Cardiff, Pettigrew was the first superintendent to write a series of articles for the *Gardeners' Chronicle* on the management of public parks.

John James Sexby (1848–1924)

J. J. Sexby was Superintendent of Parks & Gardens for the London County Council, and was responsible for the design, laying out and management of many of London's most impressive municipal parks. Until its demise in 1965, the London County Council became the chief park authority and maintained a special Parks & Open Spaces Committee, whose first chairman was the founder of the Metropolitan Public Gardens Association, Lord Meath. In 1892, a separate parks department was set up under Lt-Col. J. J. Sexby, who had formerly been employed as a surveyor of parks and open spaces by the Metropolitan Board. Yet, very little is known of John James Sexby. He is described on the title page of his book of 1898 as a lieutenant-colonel and a professional associate

J. J. Sexby.

The 1884 LCC Parks Committee.

of the Surveyors' Institution, from which it can be deduced that he probably worked as a surveyor in the Army.

Sexby's skills as a horticulturalist and garden designer cannot be doubted, and he left his mark on many of the municipal parks and gardens, about which he writes with such enthusiasm in *The Municipal Parks, Gardens and Open Spaces of London*. In it, he focuses on the municipal parks (those maintained by local authorities) rather than the nationally managed parks in central London – describing large open spaces such as Hampstead Heath as well as small, disused churchyards like that of St Dunstan's in Stepney. He was involved with such parks as Bethnal Green Gardens; Brockwell Park; Deptford Park; Dulwich Park; Eaglesfield Park; Maryon Park; Northbrook Park; Peckham Rye Park; Ruskin Park; South Park, Fulham; Springfield Park; and Wandsworth Park.

Peckham Rye Common has been a popular open space for centuries. Over the centuries, local residents battled to prevent development of the common. Finally, in 1868, Camberwell Vestry purchased the rights of the Lord of the Manor of Peckham Rye to preserve the common as a public open space. Pressure on the space led the authorities to extend the public open space by the purchase of the 51-acre Homestall farm next to the common for £51,000 in 1892. This was laid out as Peckham Rye Park by Sexby, with over

100,000 people attending its opening in May 1894. Sexby's layout catered for everyone. There were 2 acres for tennis courts, 12 acres for cricket, and 10½ acres for a children's playground around the park. Inside the park itself, there was a bowling green, a lake, ornamental flower beds, a rockery with a small grotto, an American garden, a Japanese garden, a shelter and an old English garden. There was even a whalebone arch walk, which was popular with courting couples.

The ground that became Brockwell Park was bought by the county council in 1891 and included the land with the attached Brockwell Hall. The public was admitted before the formal opening, which took place on 6 June 1892 and was performed by the county council's former chairman, Lord Roseberry. The conversion of the estate into a park was designed by Sexby with a contemporary writer approving its 'natural' appearance, who admired 'the great expanse of lawn studded with fine forest trees'. The glory of the park was the Old English Garden, which was planted within the walls of the kitchen garden. Other features of the original park mentioned by the writer of 1895 were the swimming pond, the rustic bandstand and the carpet bedding on the promenade that spelt out 'two or three bars of God save the Queen'.

Ruskin Park was another delightful example of the designs made by Lt-Col. Sexby, and was probably one of the last that he did. In this instance, the gymnastic apparatus had to be set at least 100 yards from the south and west boundaries to lessen disturbances to the inhabitants of the houses on those sides. The rest of the park was grassed and landscaped with a great variety of fine trees including cedar, oak, lime, tulip tree, Judas

The Clock Tower, Brockwell Park.

Brockwell Park, London.

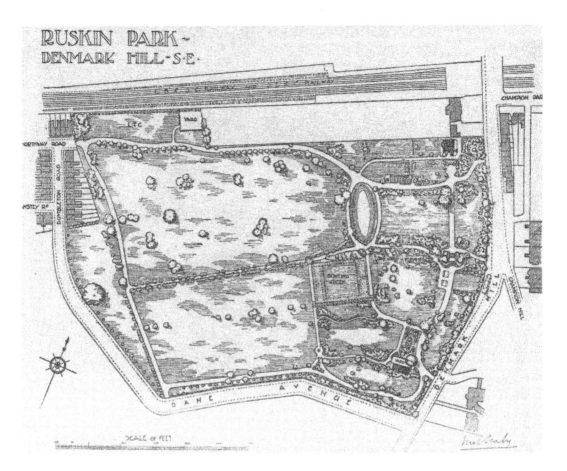

Sexby's plan for Ruskin Park.

tree and beech. The garden was charmingly designed and had as its chief ornamental feature a well-planned lake with waterfowl; the rest was planted with shrubs, bedding plants and roses. On one side, the bowling green has a handsome brick pergola planted with wisteria and climbing roses. There is also a plain wooden bandstand nearby, which is still present.

Wandsworth Park is another Sexby-designed park that retains much of his design influence. At the turn of the nineteenth century, Wandsworth was a heavily polluted suburb centred around the River Wandle, with its iron mill, brass industry and brewery. In 1897, Wandsworth District Board were given the opportunity to buy land for the purpose of laying out a public park, and they contributed £15,429 towards the purchase price of £33,000. The 8 hectares of land they were considering lay between the south bank of the River Thames and Putney Bridge Road, and at the time consisted of allotment gardens interspersed with public footpaths. The design, construction and supervision of the park was again to be allocated to Sexby, but as the purchase price of the site was more than had been expected, the construction of the park was limited to £10,000. Sexby's design for Wandsworth Park responds to two main influences current at the beginning of the twentieth century: firstly, the increase in maintenance costs and the gradual disappearance of large numbers of gardening staff, and secondly the rise in interest in

89

Rustic Bridge, Dulwich Park.

Dulwich Park.

organised sport from the 1880s onwards. Wandsworth Park was formally opened on Saturday 28 February 1903 for the use and enjoyment of the people of London forever.

At Dulwich Park, opened in June 1890, Sexby had displayed a real genius for horticulture, providing an astonishing variety of plants and gardening styles in the relatively small space available. The perimeter was planted so as to enhance the feeling of entering a rural estate. As he wrote in 1898, 'leaving now the old cottage we pass round the park, and are so shut in by the walls of trees as to quite forget the outside world'. It was to be featured in many books and it was thought in the *Gardener's Chronicle* in 1891 that: 'not even St James's Park was more skilfully laid out ... than this one under the supervision of Mr Sexby. Flowers borders, shrubberies and grass, and winding walks all nicely intermixed, so as to secure the utmost variety that the space can afford...'

Sexby eventually retired in 1910 after twenty-one years at the helm, with his impact on the parks and gardens of London as great as that of Burton, Pennethorne and Nash.

Captain Arnold Edward Sandys-Winsch (1888–1964)

Captain Arnold Edward Sandys-Winsch was born in Knutsford, Cheshire. He attended Cheshire Horticultural College, becoming a landscape architect, and was articled to the renowned landscape architect Thomas Mawson. During the First World War he was first with the Royal Field Artillery, before being attached to the Air Service as a pilot

Captain Arnold Edward
Sandys-Winsch.

91

and finally serving with the British Army of Occupation. In 1919 he became parks superintendent in Norwich – a post he held for thirty-four years. In the early 1920s, it was proposed that he use men unemployed after demobilisation to help construct some of the Norwich parks; a job he clearly carried out with dedication and meticulous attention to detail. At the time, Norwich had very few open spaces (Chapelfield Gardens was one of them), but by the time he retired Norwich had over 600 acres of parks and open spaces. Sandys-Winsch also created model allotments and organised the planting of some 20,000 trees in the parks and streets. Norwich Corporation sought to provide for the recreational needs of Norwich citizens, and the captain proved just the person to turn their vision into reality.

Because of his Army career, he seems to have taken a rather military approach to the task of creating parks in Norwich, but there is no doubt that he radically changed the appearance of Norwich and created green spaces on a huge scale for the future enjoyment of everyone.

Eaton Park was perhaps his finest park. In 1906, partly using funds raised by the Norwich Playing Fields & Open Spaces Society, the city purchased four fields of grazing land lying between the Earlham and Eaton Hall estates on the western fringes of the city. The site remained undeveloped, being used on several occasions as the site for the Royal Norfolk Agricultural Show until 1924, when proposals were put forward to develop it as a formal public park to designs by Sandys-Winsch. The years following the First World War had been a time of unemployment and hardship. Using government grants, the Corporation began to create parks as a means of providing unemployment relief. The plan at Eaton was to make a sports park. At the time, the National Playing Fields Association recommended that local authorities should adopt a minimum standard of 5 acres of public open space for every 1,000 people, 'of which at least 4 acres should be set aside for team games, tennis, bowls and children's playgrounds'. For three and a half years, over 100 men were employed to build the bandstand, pavilions and model boating and lily ponds. Tennis courts (of which there were over 40), cricket squares, bowling greens and other sports and leisure areas, as well as gardens were created. The park was officially opened by the then Prince of Wales in 1928.

At the beginning of the twentieth century, an area of land owned by the Great Hospital Trust was laid out as a park in a densely populated area of Norwich, which lay outside the old city walls. The conversion of the existing fields was completed by 1904 and the park, originally known as Catton Recreation Ground, was opened in May of that year. In the late 1920s a proposal was put forward to redevelop the site and in 1929 a design was drawn up by Sandys-Winsch. Work began in 1931 and two years later the park was reopened under the new name of Waterloo Park. It provided, within its 18 acres, grass tennis courts, football pitches, bowling greens, formal gardens, pergola walks, a pavilion, a bandstand and a children's playground, which was considered to be one of the finest in East Anglia. It was reported at its opening to have been created with the purpose of giving 'pleasure to the greatest number of people'.

Sandys-Winsch had his critics. As mentioned, he was responsible for the planting of 20,000 flowering trees in Norwich. Many said this indicated his dislike of the forest tree,

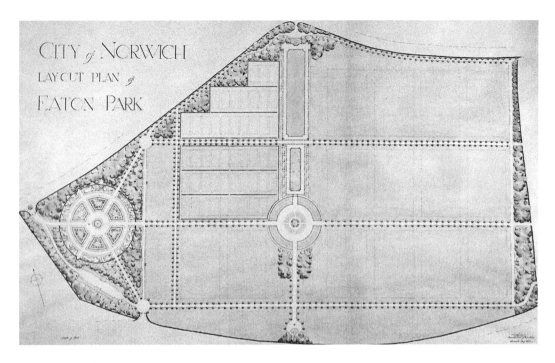

Layout plan of Eaton Park.

Eaton Park boating lake, Norwich.

which he firmly rebuked. He was often perceived as a difficult man, who was seemingly impatient with those that did not share his beliefs. Thoughts have been entertained by some that the layout of the parks and the design of their buildings – i.e. the geometric dependence of the former and the classical theme of the latter – owe something to political thinking, but this remains unproven. What is more likely is that the time

93

Sandys-Winsch spent with Thomas Mawson as a young man gave him ideas that stayed with him until he was later able to put them into practice in Norwich. What is absolutely clear about the captain's work is that in his thirty-three years as parks superintendent, he brought about a profound change in the appearance of the city and in the scale of the facilities available for the enjoyment of its citizens.

Eaton Park, Norwich.

Bibliography

Books

Anderson, A. P., *The Captain and the Norwich Parks* (Norwich: The Norwich Society, 2000).

Colquhoun, K., *The Busiest Man in England – A Life of Joseph Paxton, Gardener, Architect & Victorian Visionary* (Boston: David R. Godine, 2003).

Conway, H., *People's Parks – The Design and Development of Victorian Parks in Britain* (Cambridge: Cambridge University Press, 1991).

Craddock, J. P., *Paxton's Protégé – The Milner White Landscape Gardening Dynasty* (York: 2012).

Draper, M. P. G., *Lambeth's Open Spaces – An Historical Account* (London: London Borough of Lambeth, 1979).

Hitching, C., *Rock Landscapes – The Pulham Legacy* (Garden Art Press, 2012).

Johnson, L., *Dulwich Park – A Park for the People Forever* (Sudbury: The Lavenham Press Ltd, 2005).

Lang, A., *Saltwell Park – The Story of the People's Park* (Newcastle-upon-Tyne: Summerhill Books, 2013).

Mernick, P., *A Pictorial History of Victoria Park, London E3* (East London History Society, 1996).

Pettigrew, W. W., *Municipal Parks – Layout, Management & Administration* (London: 1929).

Rabbitts, P., *Regent's Park – From Tudor Hunting Ground to the Present* (Stroud: Amberley Publishing, 2013).

Sexby, J. J., *The Municipal Parks, Gardens & Open Spaces of London – Their History and Association* (London: 1905).

Summerson, J., *John Nash – Architect to King George IV* (London: George Allen & Unwin Ltd, 1935).

Tyack, G., *Sir James Pennethorne and the making of Victorian London* (Cambridge: Cambridge University Press, 1992).

Ullman, J., *Battersea Park* (London: Friends of Battersea Park, 2016).

Waymark, J., *Thomas Mawson – Life, Gardens and Landscapes* (London: Frances Lincoln Ltd, 2009).

Whitbourn, P., *Decimus Burton Esquire – Architect and Gentleman (1800–1881)* (The Royal Tunbridge Wells Civic Society, 2006).

Websites

www.historicengland.org.uk

www.londongardenstrust.org

www.oxforddnb.com

www.parksandgardens.org